marimekko

Art of print making since 1951

PARACHUTE

Home essentials for your natural habitat.

KINFOLK

MAGAZINE	EDITOR-IN-CHIEF	John Clifford Burns
	EDITOR	Harriet Fitch Little
	ART DIRECTOR	Christian Møller Andersen
	DESIGN DIRECTOR	Alex Hunting
	COPY EDITOR	Rachel Holzman
	FACT CHECKER	Gabriele Dellisanti
	EDITORIAL INTERNS	Natalia Lauritzen
		Benjamin Tarp

STUDIO	COMMERCIAL DIRECTOR	Mads Westendahl
	ADVERTISING DIRECTOR	Jessica Gray
	SALES & DISTRIBUTION DIRECTOR	Edward Mannering
	STUDIO & PROJECT MANAGER	Susanne Buch Petersen
	DESIGNER & ART DIRECTOR	Staffan Sundström
	PRODUCER	Cecilie Jegsen
	CO-FOUNDER	Nathan Williams

STYLING, HAIR & MAKEUP

Sade Akin Boyewa El, Eloise Cheung, Ben Clark, Jermaine Daley, Taan Doan, Jordy Huinder, Javier Irigoyen, Fatimot Isadare, Lisa Jahovic, Roberta Kearsey, Tomihiro Kono, Tamara Laureus, Pernilla Löfberg, Maiko Mano, Rommy Najor, David Nolan, Giulio Panciera, Tania Rat-Patron, Rebecca Rojas, Sandy Suffield, Agus Suga, Camille-Joséphine Teisseire, Lana Turner, Mieko Yoshioka

WORDS

Alex Anderson, Rima Sabina Aouf, Katie Calautti, James Clasper, Djassi DaCosta Johnson, Stephanie d'Arc Taylor, Daphnée Denis, Tom Faber, Jessica Furseth, Bella Gladman, Selena Hoy, Robert Ito, David Keenan, Ana Kinsella, Stevie Mackenzie-Smith, Kyla Marshell, Sean Michaels, Megan Nolan, Hettie O'Brien, Debika Ray, Tristan Rutherford, Laura Rysman, Caspar Salmon, Rhian Sasseen, Ben Shattuck, Rachel Syme, Pip Usher

PHOTOGRAPHY

Gustav Almestål, Ted Belton, Tom Bianchi, Michaël Borremans, Luc Braquet, James Carriere, Claire Cottrell, Pelle Crépin, Diane Dal-Pra, Lauren Dukoff, Luke Evans, Gelcream, Marsý Hild Þórsdóttir, Myoung Ho Lee, Cecilie Jegsen, Charlotte Lapalus, Romain Laprade, Michael Oliver Love, Mar + Vin, Christian Møller Andersen, Jum Nakao, Vincent Ricci, Pia Riverola, Dominik Tarabanski, Aaron Tilley, Zoltan Tombor, Hanna Tveite, Andre D. Wagner, Johanna Wallin, Jun Yasui

CROSSWORD	Anna Gundlach
PUBLICATION DESIGN	Alex Hunting Studio
COVER PHOTOGRAPH	Romain Laprade

Kinfolk (ISSN 2596-6154) is published quarterly by Ouur ApS, Amagertorv 14, 1, 1160 Copenhagen, Denmark. Printed by Taylor Bloxham Limited in Leicester, United Kingdom. Color reproduction by PH Media in Roche, United Kingdom. All rights reserved. No part of this publication may be reproduced, distributed or transmitted in any form or by any means, including photocopying or other electronic or mechanical methods, without prior written permission of the editor-in-chief, except in the case of brief quotations embodied in critical reviews and certain other noncommercial uses permitted by copyright law. The US annual subscription price is $87 USD. Airfreight and mailing in the USA by Worldnet Shipping Inc., 156-15, 146th Avenue, 2nd Floor, Jamaica, NY 11434, USA. Application to mail at periodicals postage prices is pending at Jamaica NY 11431. US Postmaster: send address changes to Kinfolk, Worldnet Shipping Inc., 156-15, 146th Avenue, 2nd Floor, Jamaica, NY 11434, USA. Subscription records are maintained at Ouur ApS, Amagertorv 14, 1, 1160 Copenhagen, Denmark. The views expressed in Kinfolk magazine are those of the respective contributors and are not necessarily shared by the company or its staff. SUBSCRIBE: Kinfolk is published four times a year. To subscribe, visit www.kinfolk.com/subscribe or email us at info@kinfolk.com. CONTACT US: If you have questions or comments, please write to us at info@kinfolk.com. For advertising inquiries, get in touch at advertising@kinfolk.com. For partnerships and business opportunities, contact mads@kinfolk.com

Starters

12 – 40

Features

42 – 112

"The tree leaves present themselves as their own performance."
LANA TURNER – P.86

Photograph: Romain Laprade

Change

Directory

114 – 176

178 – 192

"I loved the prospect of one day making the changes I had dreamed about."
LINDSAY PEOPLES WAGNER – P.114

Photograph: Zoltan Tombor

marset

Taking care of light

For every positive gain attributed to the idea of change, such as self-improvement, bold adventuring or collective hope, there often follows the very human instinct to feel quite the opposite: fear, self-doubt and loss. How best to navigate these conflicting forces?

When, at the age of 40, Shahira Fahmy decided she wanted to take a break from architecture to become an actress, she took comfort in a pithy quote she heard attributed to Swiss psychiatrist Carl Jung: "Life really does begin at 40. Up until then, you are just doing research."

But if there's one thing we learned while putting together the Change section of this issue, it's that there's no real way of predicting when we'll suddenly be confronted with a new pathway in life. For Fahmy, it was a project to design a film set landing on her desk that would eventually lead her to walk the red carpet at the Cannes Film Festival. For John Urschel, it was suffering a major concussion that sparked a new direction; worried about his future playing football in the NFL, he revived his childhood love of math and switched his goals to those of career academia. And for Lindsay Peoples Wagner, a new start came quite abruptly; in 2018, she was called into a meeting at Condé Nast and offered the position of editor-in-chief at *Teen Vogue*.

Fittingly, for the Change issue, we've made some leaps into the unknown. The Borrowers, on page 168, is our first-ever fashion shoot featuring children; they had a ball playing dress-up with adult-sized clothes. Elsewhere, we interviewed (and styled) Ai-Da, a successful early-career artist who also happens to be a robot. Of the many sorts of change approached in this issue, the shift toward AI may be the most fundamental to our shared future. In our feature profile we meet Greta Lee, the actress on the verge of becoming a producer of her own show. She talks about how the lack of substantial parts for Korean Americans compelled her to start writing scripts. Lee finds humor in the fact that she now works with the same suits who she once waited on at restaurants: "*I have served you pork buns, sir.*"

You'll notice that *Kinfolk* has had something of a spring-cleaning. We've introduced more essays in the Starters section of the magazine, plus a roster of new formats in the Directory, including an interview spot where people talk about their favorite object, and another where we quiz them about what they did last night. Design-minded readers should also keep their eyes peeled for a number of tweaks we've made to the issue.

JOHN CLIFFORD BURNS & HARRIET FITCH LITTLE

Mitchell Gold
+Bob Williams

SPRING 2020

HANDCRAFTED IN NORTH CAROLINA

1.

Starters

60 — 125

Neither Here Nor There

In praise of being in-between.

To be in transit is to navigate a void between points of departure and arrival. When we're in an airplane, untethered to the earth, time and space roll by indifferently. Only seldom does a vague sense of location present itself through the oval window—green irrigation circles printed on the Plains, dotted lines of city light woven in the darkness, black granite peaks locked in ice.

On road trips, these captivating pauses come at shorter intervals between the on- and off-ramps, at gas stations, diners and cheap motels. Jack Kerouac's unspooling tale, *On the Road*, follows his vision of "one great red line across America," but gathers its tone and value in the dingy waysides of the route. It begins inauspiciously, with rain coming down hard at Bear Mountain Bridge on Route 6. Waiting alone for a ride at an abandoned filling station, looking toward the "so-longed-for west," Kerouac finds himself already in the daunting nowhere of that bold line.

It's hard to explain the melancholy allure of that lonely spot—the mossy dripping of rainwater, the tired gas pumps, the "closed" sign askew in a blind window, the empty road. Later, in a dim bus station café somewhere between Chicago and Denver, Kerouac watches a waitress at work and cheerfully eats apple pie and ice cream. "That's practically all I ate all the way across the country," he remarks. And still later in a "gloomy old Plains inn of a hotel" he wakens in a liminal place to "the strangest moment": "I was far away from home... and I looked at the cracked high ceiling and really didn't know who I was for about fifteen strange seconds... I was halfway across America at the dividing line between the East of my youth and the West of my future."[1]

Kerouac's vivid, anxious episode in transit contrasts with others' more upbeat accounts of in-between places. Architect Herman Hertzberger praises "the habitable spaces between things"—doorsteps, stoops, landings, balconies, porches—for their ability to accommodate unscripted pauses and chance meetings. Sociologist Ray Oldenburg lauds "third places"—the places we frequent between work and home—for their unpretentious communality and cheerful banter over a cold beer or hot coffee and tasty food.[2] These happy between places brighten everyday routines.

Kerouac illustrates the more profound shades of stopovers between destinations. He shows that in them we momentarily become strangers to our ordered selves, acutely aware of other places, other people. Dusky, unfamiliar rooms become thresholds to other possibilities; accents and habits of others become not merely the mannerisms of strangers but the colorful, disorienting reflections of who we might have become in their places. There's an appeal to the convenience of getting quickly from one place to another, to inattentively traversing the tiresome distance between destinations. But the meaning of travel deepens at the wayside stops, where life can take on enthralling hues and unanticipated values.

Words by Alex Anderson

NOTES

1. Liminal space is often associated with creativity. This applies to life transitions, as well as physical journeys. From *Catcher in the Rye* to the Britney Spears film *Crossroads*, coming-of-age stories thrill us because they catch their protagonists at a point when they've left childhood behind but not yet found their adult selves.

2. An important caveat to Oldenburg's love of "third spaces" is that he only sees them as valuable if they exist within a pre-defined physical community. Indeed, he decries how suburban sprawl and the expanding commuter belt have robbed neighborhoods of the local pubs in which they would have previously socialized.

Noticeably Absent

On the power of unseen characters.

Of all the unseen characters in literature, one of the most interesting is Mr. Perry, the doctor in Jane Austen's *Emma*. Perry, who never actually appears in the novel, is alluded to often, and his wisdom is constantly cited by Emma's hypochondriacal father. Along with the book's other background characters, he deepens the world Austen evokes by giving texture to the village of Highbury; he also furthers the plot and allows Austen to get in a little dig at the growing popularity of physicians at the time.

Movies often use unseen characters, and the device is particularly effective since film is a visual medium, where everything else is presented outright. Absence can hang heavily over proceedings, as we see in Hitchcock's ingenious adaptation of Daphne du Maurier's novel *Rebecca*. Rebecca's beauty was legendary, but we only glimpse it in a portrait displayed on the landing of Manderley. By existing in our imagination, the off-screen character has a terribly powerful aura—in contrast to the prosaically real people we see depicted. In the film this adds to the suggestion of Rebecca's sensuality, and keeps the past out of reach—two factors that make her lingering image so intriguing.

The idea of the unseen character as a symbol is front and center in Samuel Beckett's play *Waiting for Godot*, where the perpetually anticipated Godot stands, perhaps, for the absurdity of our existence. Only our imagination is up to the job of conceiving of so transcendent a personality. Beckett makes his onstage characters especially earthbound, in order to clash with such pregnant imagery.

Off-screen characters have also been used to illustrate the battle of the sexes. In the classic British sitcom *Dad's Army*, the wives and partners of the soldiers are never seen, while in George Cukor's scintillating 1939 comedy *The Women*, adapted from a play by Clare Boothe Luce, no men ever appear. This gives a sense of characters manipulating action in the background, but it also removes sexuality (in a predominantly heterosexual world) from the dynamic between characters, which perhaps enables them to get the business of comedy nailed down more effectively. In *Dad's Army*, the absence of Captain Mainwaring's wife suggests that she is the person pulling all the strings behind the scenes, and lends an air of trifling absurdity to the captain's endeavors. But in *The Women*, we do not get a sense of male partners being all-powerful. The film eradicates men entirely, as a nuisance almost: In a heavily patriarchal society, this is a conscious choice that pokes fun at men's opinion of themselves.

When we consider unseen characters, our imaginations throw a sort of gauze of mystery over the all-too-real elements we perceive; we can conceive of these people so vividly that they easily lock step with the fictional worlds they never enter. Off-screen characters represent a tussle between the concrete and the intangible—and in grappling with that tension, we actually participate in the art we are consuming. *Words by Caspar Salmon*

Left Photograph: Ludvig Röm. Stylist: Hilda Sandström. Art Direction: Öström Studio. Courtesy of Inabo. Right Photograph: Hanna Tveite

LET IT SLIP

by Pip Usher

There's a scene in *Curb Your Enthusiasm* where Larry gets off on the wrong foot with his host for refusing to take his sneakers off in their home. As the ensuing fracas proves, the etiquette around outdoor footwear can be fraught. Could slippers be the solution? From Japan to Serbia, many countries consider it customary to wear slippers at home and—for added points—to offer a pair to guests, too. For those who prefer to slip on their own pair, online forums reveal that ballet-style slippers are an easily portable choice. Will you raise eyebrows when you remove them from your bag? Perhaps—but you'll still be more popular than the person with muddy soles. *Slippers by Inabo*

Modern Fancy

The humble origins of high-end food.

Oysters—which used to be sourced from river beds as cheap sustenance for impoverished workers—are now washed down with Champagne. Quinoa, a staple grain from the Andes, has become a costly commodity. Even caviar, a delicacy favored by the Russian elite, was once served as a free bar snack in American saloons in the hope that its saltiness would encourage drinking. If we can learn anything from these once-humble goodies, it's that even the least glamorous can succeed with the right rebrand.

It turns out that a savvy reinvention, coupled with diminished availability, can transform even the shoddiest reputation. When early settlers first arrived on America's East Coast, they had such an abundant supply of lobster that it became the diet of the poverty-stricken and the incarcerated. Even prisons limited their servings to once a week because of the perceived cruelty of making people eat it. But when railways began to expand across America, train managers realized that they could repackage this lowly protein and serve it to unsuspecting Midwesterners who wouldn't know any better. Gradually, people developed a taste for it.

Post–World War II, lobster assumed its status as a luxury item enjoyed by those wealthy enough to pay market rate for it. It was now boiled alive—a method that reduced the risk of food poisoning—and had become synonymous with an upper-crust New England lifestyle. Dwindling lobster stocks had driven the price up, but its radical new identity also proved the power of shrewd marketing. Diners weren't just enjoying the taste of its meat. They were also buying into the fantasy that surrounded it.

In the case of the caviar-producing sturgeon fish, a waning population was responsible for the roe becoming a rarity. But for most delicacies, their newfound desirability is more a reflection of changing fashions than simple economics. We all like to feel fancy—the trick is convincing people that a simple food item is capable of doing that. *Words by Pip Usher*

Kyle Chayka

A conversation about the affectations of austere aesthetics.

Photograph: Vincent Ricci, Location: Edo-Tokyo Open Air Museum

Kyle Chayka's new book, *The Longing for Less: Living with Minimalism*, is the latest in a raft of publications about reducing physical and mental clutter. But unlike, say, Marie Kondo, Chayka doesn't care what the inside of your closet looks like. "My writing is a tool for self-awareness, for myself as much as for a reader," says the author, who remains a sharp and self-reflective critic of minimalism as a lifestyle trend. Here, he tells Stephanie d'Arc Taylor how we need to start thinking about what we're consuming, and why.

SDT: *Do you think the human impulse to accumulate has always existed or is it a product of our modern age?* **KC:** I think both consumerism and accumulation have existed for a very long time. But now people may be realizing that buying more stuff isn't making them happier. We've been told that the possessions we have and the things we buy are the root of our identities. Because we've been alienated from the things that really matter, like the products of our labor, our creative practices and our family or friends by this super-consumerist culture, we have to find an alternative. Minimalism becomes a way of being in the world.

SDT: *So will we find peace if we eschew all earthly treasures?* **KC:** It's about balance between appreciation for the material and recognition that accumulation can be unfulfilling. In Heian-era Japan, people loved to get new robes and try new incense and admire the new cherry blossoms. But this mingled with the Buddhist philosophy of trying to get beyond desire. That balance between the two is the most important.

SDT: *Is minimalism just another lifestyle trend, like gluten-free diets or CrossFit?* **KC:** CrossFit is actually a really good comparison; minimalism can be thought of as a fitness or wellness habit for your mind or your space. It's a way of becoming more mindful and aware of what's around you. As a trend, it represents an attitude people started having around the financial crisis.

SDT: *Is minimalism only accessible to the wealthy, à la Thoreau, who managed to "live simply" because his mother was preparing his meals and doing his laundry?* **KC:** It's often very expensive to practice minimalism. Wealthier people always know they can buy new things. They don't face the same precariousness as poorer people, which makes you hold onto your possessions tighter.

SDT: *Do you find that people who practice minimalism can be rather smug about it?* **KC:** Yeah, I think the affectation of minimalism becomes a way to set yourself apart from the people or society around you. What is the ultimate luxury good when you already have everything? Getting rid of stuff. It's the endpoint of a super-consumerist life: to move beyond the actual stuff and access that smug feeling about not needing things.

SDT: *Do you feel that minimalism is incorrectly thought of as an aesthetic in itself, rather than an approach?* **KC:** I keep trying to get back to the idea rather than the stuff. Today's prevalence of advertising means we're sold things all the time, told to focus on brands, personal brands, product brands. Many people think of minimalism as a series of products that you buy, but the true attitude of minimalism is not about material things, it's about a way of living. It's about focusing on your sensory perception, having a radically open attitude to the world. You're not radically open if you will only have one kind of chair in your house, if you'll only have blond wood furniture. Through the book, I get to the idea that the contemporary lifestyle interpretation of minimalism is about controlling the things around you, but the true minimalist attitude is embracing the lack of control.

SDT: *What would I find if I showed up unannounced at your house?* **KC:** Our bedroom is unbelievably messy! Our suitcases are always open on the floor because we travel too much. Most of our furniture is, yes, mid-century modern from a vintage store in DC. There are a lot of books everywhere. I do think carefully before I buy something, partly for budgeting reasons, but also because I want everything to go together. That's my own minimalist mania.
Interview by Stephanie d'Arc Taylor

In his book, Chayka writes about how many of the Westerners who disseminated minimalist principles —including Mies van der Rohe, John Cage and Agnes Martin— were influenced by Japanese aesthetics.

THE OLD SCHOOL

by Pip Usher

First, there was the slow food movement. Now, that commitment to a more thoughtful life has been applied to children's toys. Eschewing the garish, battery-operated gimmicks of their contemporaries, slow toys take a sweetly nostalgic approach to playtime. Train sets, building blocks, and Lego all sit within the category of toys that encourage little ones to entertain themselves in an imaginative and unstructured way. Such free play, as it's known, is vital for children's cognitive development—studies point to its role in helping them learn to self-regulate their emotions and behavior. Framed in that context, slow toys seem to be a win-win: not only do they encourage maturity, but the house might be quieter, too. *Toys by Yan Ruilin*

Out of Your Depth

In defense of late learners.

The purple gentian is an unassuming wildflower that emerges in the cold November sun. Amenable to harsh conditions, it brightly carries on when other flowers have long since disappeared. Emily Dickinson, the American botanist better known as a poet, wrote admiringly about the gentian—"The frosts were her condition"—and claimed it as a vital emblem of her own late development. In her poems, the gentian proclaims that the late bloomer comes tardily, but shines gloriously in adversity.

For most people, however, there is nothing glorious in having to wait too long for success or in taking on mundane challenges that others overcame long ago. A 30-year-old wobbling unsteadily on a bicycle or floundering in the shallow end of a swimming pool is hardly the ravishing late bloomer Dickinson envisioned. Sometimes it seems like the only real adversities the late-blooming bike rider or swimmer faces are frustration and humiliation. If kids can learn this stuff, why can't I? But these aren't the only challenges. Anyone who has learned to ride a bike late in life knows that adults simply fall farther, harder and more painfully than children do. Gravity conspires against ambition.

The mind conspires against ambition too. Brain researchers at MIT have recently discovered that adults' "superior cognitive function"—their focus and memory—actually makes it difficult for them to learn the subtleties of a new language. This is because adults' well-developed capacity to acquire and analyze information dominates more fluid, unconscious styles of learning that develop earlier in life. Kids learn languages—and skills like bike riding—so easily because they don't think about it too much. They just do it.

There is hope for the late bloomer: That same fluid ability is still there beneath the embarrassment and overthinking. So it is worth following the advice of the late-starting "guy who can ride a bike," sportswriter Barry Petchesky: "Here's the secret to learning to ride a bike: *Just keep trying it, you'll get it soon.*" Substitute learning to ski, to swim, to drive, to watercolor—you get the idea—and you too can be, like the purple gentian, a ravishing late bloomer.

Words by Alex Anderson

Left Photography: Courtesy of Yan Ruilin. Right Photograph: *Swimming to Careyes* by Tom Bianchi, 1992. Courtesy of Fahey/Klein Gallery

Photograph: Johanna Wallin

Word: Flygskam

Can a new sort of shame slow air travel?

Etymology: Swedish singer-songwriter Staffan Lindberg announced in 2017 that he would no longer use air travel, a decision co-signed by other Swedish public figures including opera singer Malena Ernman (Greta Thunberg's mother) and the Olympic athlete Björn Ferry. The neologism *flygskam* has gained popularity in the years since, combining the Swedish words for flight and shame.

Meaning: Flygskam refers to the particular anti-flying movement that grew out of Sweden. But it also relates to the more general and subjective issue of guilt that an individual may feel around their carbon footprint and air travel. It is hoped that an atmosphere of disapproval toward frequent fliers will gradually shift attitudes and decrease the normalization of commercial flying.

The other Scandinavian words that have captured English-speaking interest also tend to be lifestyle-related. *Hygge*, of course, denotes a particular brand of self-care coziness. *Lagom* describes something which achieves perfect balance and moderation. Is flygskam to be bracketed with those words—a highly brandable and middle-class concern? It's true that wealthier people are more likely to have the time and money to reject budget airlines and choose days spent on trains. Notably, flygskam has given birth to another word, *tågskryt*, meaning train brag. Shame works as a deterrent only some of the time. Fat-shaming doesn't decrease obesity, making it nothing but pointlessly cruel. Telling a smoker they ought to be ashamed of hurting themselves is not effective, but warning them that smoking hurts other people can be. Perhaps this tells us that flygskam will be a successful movement if it is a positive, optimistic step toward community, rather than an attempt to induce personal guilt.

Words by Megan Nolan

Alexandre Mattiussi

Meet the French fashion designer who just wants to be friends.

They say you cannot choose your family, but you can choose your friends. Alexandre Mattiussi would like you to choose him—or rather his label AMI, a contraction of his initials and the last letter of his name (it means "friend" in French). The 39-year-old designer, an alum of Dior, Givenchy and Marc Jacobs, launched his first menswear collection in January 2011[1] with the promise of making fashion more approachable, and has since become a global player with stores in Paris, London, Tokyo, Hong Kong, Beijing and Chengdu.[2] Now, as the Parisian house ventures into womenswear, Mattiussi maintains a down-to-earth approach to his craft and, he insists, one goal: to be happy.

DD: *Does "friendly fashion" sum up your brand's philosophy?* **AM:** Yes, as soon as I realized that my initials formed the word "ami," I felt it suited me. And when I started developing an interest in fashion, I immediately thought that it would be a great brand name. Clothes are intimate—we get into people's closets—but there's a commercial side too. I like the idea of *commerce de proximité*, local commerce. People aren't paying an arm and a leg for a 4,000-euro T-shirt, but we're still talking about quality products that they spend a certain sum of money on, and I respect that a lot. When I design a garment, I always think about the person who will wear it, a little like a baker makes his baguette knowing a client will buy it to make toast for breakfast. Some designers are not in fashion because they want to dress people, but the premise of AMI is straightforward: I want to draw clothes that me and my friends want to wear and that we can afford. That's the deal.

Photography: Luc Braquet

Mattiussi donates all profits from the sale of AMI's red beanie hat to French organization Sidaction, which raises awareness and funds for those living with HIV or AIDS.

NOTES

1. Mattiussi closed down an earlier form of the business in 2002 but, following a meeting with Marc Jacobs' CEO Bertrand Stalla-Bourdillon, was convinced he could give AMI a second try in 2011—providing he had a strong team to support him.

2. "Having an idea, being creative, isn't the hardest part," Mattiussi says of his business. "The hardest part is setting everything up so that it actually happens, that it ends up on a rack, in a shop."
—
—

I'm not making clothes so they end up hanging in a museum. I'm a normal designer—I like saying that.

DD: *How do you want the AMI customer to feel in your clothes?* **AM:** I try to work around the ideal wardrobe, relatively speaking of course, but something that feels essential. I like the idea of a garment that fits everyone, that most people love. A garment that is well cut, well-constructed, that feels right. AMI is a brand that you recommend through word of mouth, like you would a good restaurant. I enjoy not being mainstream, not having a thousand stores around the world. AMI is a brand that you have to discover and choose. I like that it's democratic and confidential at the same time.

DD: *As a child, you considered becoming a professional ballet dancer, but you've said that you realized you hated competing with others after trying out for the Opéra de Paris. Do you still feel that way?* **AM:** I was a French Billy Elliot. I was always dancing with my girlfriends, which was quite unusual for a little boy from Normandie back in the 1980s. At 14, I decided to try out for the Opéra de Paris, and suddenly found myself in a room with another 500 children who were ready to kill in order to succeed. The energy was so violent—it wasn't something I'd encountered before. I got out of there and thought: "This isn't for me." I still feel the same. I've never sought to measure myself against others. My only goal is to be happy in what I do and to do things for people rather than against them.

DD: *What kind of person is a good fit for your team?* **AM:** I'm very intuitive when it comes to hiring. I don't really look at CVs. I look for professionalism, talent and energy, but we have a lot of fun too. I love my team because they're all very different from one another. They don't fit one single profile. In the past, I worked for fashion houses where we all looked alike because the artistic director who hired us had only one kind of person in mind and it felt like we were an army of clones. I've known places where we were seriously bored and scared. I promised myself that when I had my own brand, nobody would have a knot in their stomach coming into work. I'm happy, because I've achieved that. My team's energy is amazing.

DD: *You're a menswear designer by trade. How did the transition into womenswear happen?* **AM:** I'm surrounded by women. Half of my team are women, I have my girlfriends, my mother…Very quickly, these women adopted our men's wardrobe, so eventually, I decided to create a collection for them. At first, I called it "menswear for women," because it was a continuation of the men's wardrobe and because I wanted to take it slow. It wouldn't have made sense for me to suddenly present dresses and high heels. Out of humility, I wanted to take my time to start this conversation with the AMI woman. And that woman helps me so much, she challenges me, she makes me see the AMI man that I built nine years ago differently.

DD: *How so?* **AM:** I've been working in menswear for 20 years, so I have one kind of body in mind, proportions, sleeve lengths… All of a sudden, with women, I need to approach the garment differently—it doesn't fit the same way. And that also makes me see menswear with new eyes, with more tenderness. For instance, we usually design the men's collection first, and later decide what can be adapted into womenswear. But for our most recent collection, we started designing for women first, so it was womenswear that became an inspiration for the menswear this time around.

DD: *What lessons did you learn from past positions at Dior, Givenchy, Marc Jacobs?* **AM:** Dior was my first real experience. It was mainly observation, because I was straight out of school, where you learn how to be creative but not how to be a designer. Givenchy was a fundamental experience for me. It's where I really learned the ins and outs of the job—how to build a collection from A to Z and how to work with others, because a designer never works in isolation. With Marc Jacobs… You learn from everything of course, but that job mostly made me realize that I was ready to tell my own story.

DD: *Is it true that, during a job interview, you once said that your ambition in life is to be happy?* **AM:** Yes. I said that being happy was the only thing that mattered, whether I'm rich or poor, alone or not… And it totally shocked them. I'm proud of my answer, because I would have been miserable in a place where you're not allowed to voice that. Today, I've found my happiness in AMI. I'm happy to build this story that keeps growing, with a team I adore and with clients around the world wearing my clothes. I'm always touched when I see someone wearing my designs. I've followed people in the street to make sure that it's really my clothes they're wearing. *Interview by Daphnée Denis*

> "*I'm always touched when I see someone wearing my designs. I've followed people in the street to make sure that it's really my clothes they're wearing.*"

"I'm not a clothes revolutionary,
I like to approach things slowly,"
says Mattiussi of his design process.

MADE WITH LOVE
by Harriet Fitch Little

The AMI logo—which consists of the letter A, topped with a heart—is descended from a childhood doodle by Mattiussi that he adopted as his signature when writing letters to loved ones. Christened the "ami de coeur"—which translates as friend of hearts—this playful twist on the ace of hearts is intended to communicate AMI's overarching desire to approach fashion in a more friendly way.

KONAMI

Manufactured by Erik Jørgensen, designed by Damian Williamson.

Konami reveals a perfectly balanced symbiosis of artistic vision and skill. At first glance, the sofa appears to be a minimalistic piece of furniture, but upon closer inspection, designer Damian Williamson's stylistic waves and organic curves set the scene. The elegant lines of Konami is reflected in Kumo - the sculptural side table also designed by Williamson.

ERIK **Jørgensen**

ERIK JØRGENSEN   SHOWROOM   BREDGADE 76   1260 COPENHAGEN K   TLF. +45 86 21 53 00

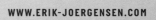

WWW.ERIK-JOERGENSEN.COM

Spaceship House

The mothership of Googie architecture.

The Spaceship House, built in California by architect Mary Gordon, is a place that E.T. could call home: It's a curvaceous white beacon topped by TV-shaped towers and encircled by an outdoor staircase that looks like a radar dish.[1]

It could only have been built in the 1970s. Back then, the United States faced the twin specters of war and recession. These grim prospects forced some into spiritualism and yoga (Iyengar and Ashtanga both put down roots during that decade) while others sought solace in astronomy and acid. Architecture, music and film (see *Close Encounters of the Third Kind* and *Invasion of the Body Snatchers*) followed the Space Age trend.[2] NASA became so confident of finding extraterrestrial life that it blasted a gold-plated record into outer space containing a map to earth and a message from Jimmy Carter. Let's hope E.T. hadn't already upgraded to cassette.

Architectural futurism is all about embracing the unknown. While Frank Gehry's Guggenheim Museum in Bilbao, Spain could conceivably message aliens, it also bends glass and titanium to cast a 21st-century cathedral within. Perhaps if we earthlings want to think outside the box about our own dismal prospects, we'd do well to follow the futurists' lead and imagine bolder, less boxy, buildings.

Words by Tristan Rutherford

NOTES

1. Although the Spaceship House looks like a sizeable building, its wacky proportions and extremely thick, curved walls mean that indoor space is limited. Speaking to Apartment Therapy in 2016, its then-occupier Angelina Rennell (daughter of architect Cynthia) admitted there wasn't room for a single closet.

2. Space Age (also known as "Googie") architecture waned in popularity shortly after the Spaceship House was completed in 1972. Apollo 11's successful moon landing represented the culmination of a feverishly fought Space Race, and architects turned their attention towards more organic, earthbound forms.

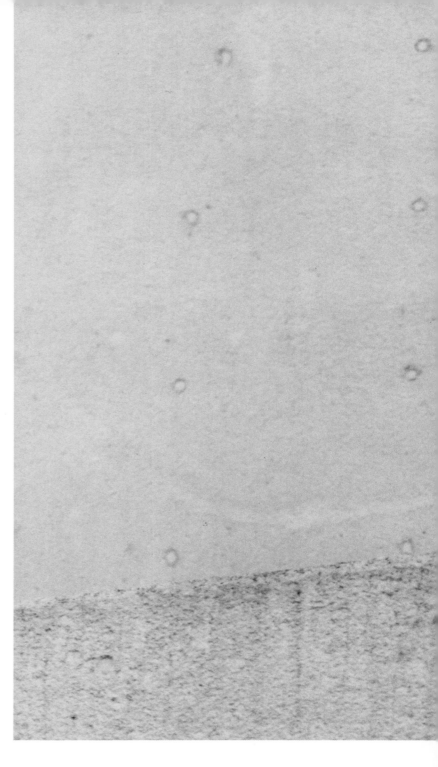

Mieko Kawakami

Meet the rising author who already longs for obsolescence.

Mieko Kawakami writes about women and gender, but she wishes society would progress to a point where she didn't have to. In 2008 she won the Akutagawa Prize, arguably Japan's most prestigious literary award, for her novella *Chichi to Ran*, or Breasts and Eggs, which explores body image in modern Japan through the relationships between a girl, her mother and her aunt. Kawakami expanded the story into a novel, which will be published in English by Picador in spring 2020. When we meet under the spaceship-like shadow of the Edo-Tokyo museum, Haruki Murakami's favorite young writer talks about the gender gap, memory and the Osaka dialect.

SH: *You've written about a nostalgia for your school years. What formative experiences from your youth have you carried into your writing?* **MK:** Until I was about 30, I never thought I'd be able to make a living as a writer. But thinking about it now, my childhood sense, my discomfort at the time, the strangeness—for example—of a landscape that left a really strong impression, that is all directly related to my current work. Of

Photograph: Jun Yasui, Makeup: Mieko Yoshioka

Mieko Kawakami is pictured at the Edo-Tokyo Museum—a museum dedicated to exploring the history of Tokyo during the Edo (or Tokugawa) period from 1603 to 1868, commonly considered the last epoch of traditional Japan.

the things that scared or surprised me as a child, their sense of strangeness gets stronger every year.

SH: *You previously had a career as a musician. What role does music play in your written work?* **MK:** I think what I've learned most from music is rhythm. I was born in Osaka and have the Osaka dialect accent, which is very melodious. For example, during Buddhist incantations, Tokyoites read it straight, but Osakans sound almost drunk—or like they're really *feeling* it. That kind of musicality affects how we think about things, and how melodic dialogues are spoken. We can't separate music from it.

SH: *Do you have any writing rituals?* **MK:** I decide on the music first of all. Then I make plenty of burdock tea—it's delicious. The scene I'm writing is connected to the music, and then whenever I'm writing and I play that music, I can enter the scene. That's my little magic.

SH: *You examine the nature of memory in several of your works. What draws you to this?* **MK:** The identity of our self is memory. Of course, if we lose our memory, self still exists, but it is strange to think that there is no such thing as a complete loss of memory. For humans, memory is a huge mystery. I'm 43 years old, but I can only recall a really small amount of time from my 43 years. There might be a memory that left a deep impression on me, but the person next to me may have forgotten it. It has that kind of a strange existence. Memory is a huge source of imagination within fiction.

SH: *What kind of relationship do you hope your readers will have with your work?* **MK:** I write about women in Japan—a country that has a severe gender gap. There is no meaningful sex education in Japan, and gender education in general is lagging—there's a really deep-seated impression that women are here for the pleasure of men. A lot of young people read my writing with a heavy heart. But when people read my books [in the future], I want them to say, "Mieko's books are no longer necessary for young people." Instead of relating to the painful feelings, if my books became unnecessary, that would be the best thing. Men, women and other-gendered people will focus on the next literary topic and on a wider view. I want to see that kind of maturity. *Interview by Selena Hoy*

Why flower power is perennial in the spring.

When *The Devil Wears Prada*'s Miranda Priestly issued her withering fashion world put-down: "Florals? For spring? Groundbreaking," she intimated that the seasonal taking-up of florals is, well, less than imaginative. But this annual ritual is not to be sneered at—it's what we do. Who can resist those early blooms: the first snowdrops and the first daffodils, pushing up through hard ground, bursting forth with the desire to exist once again after a long winter. Clothing contains the same promise. A fluid midi dress in a wildflower print is a one-way ticket out of the relentless confines of outerwear and central heating, finally. This feeling runs back to the Romans. At Floralia—the spring festival in honor of Flora, goddess of flowers and fertility—white robes were eschewed in favor of bright colors and over-the-top floral displays. Crowds were pelted with flowers in celebration of the new year's early abundance. And so fashion designers find ways to remake florals anew. Somehow, they still manage to make them appear original. At Balenciaga, Demna Gvasalia's were transformed through head-to-toe spandex for SS17. Dries Van Noten's were photographed from his garden roses and dahlias to make beauty more "direct," and Cecilie Bahnsen's silhouettes evoke the bell-shaped flowers that bees adore. Florals for spring is a form of thanksgiving. It's in our nature.
Words by Stevie Mackenzie-Smith

Left Photograph: Pia Riverola, Right Photograph: Courtesy of Cecilie Bahnsen

For his *Tree* series, photographer Myoung Ho Lee erected white canvas backdrops behind solitary trees.

The path ahead is dark. A tree canopy seals off the sky, each leaf rendered so vividly it almost looks real. Gravel crunches underfoot. Your pursuers cannot be far behind. In front, the path splits in two. To the left, a starlit lake gleams in the distance, a single rowboat bobbing invitingly by the shore. On your right is a dead end, a wall rising abruptly from the undergrowth. Which way do you go?

Any seasoned video gamer would turn right. If one path is obviously designed to take you onward in the game's narrative, you take the other: It's where the treasure is hidden. No matter how counterintuitive it feels, you learn to go the wrong way first. Since most games are designed with linear narratives—a single route leading to a single ending—the wrong path is actually just the scenic route. So take a detour and investigate the forest. You'll still end up at the lake. We all get to the end, one way or another.

Games are like life—and unlike books or films—in that *you* are the protagonist, responsible for your own decisions. The difference, of course, is that those decisions have no real consequences, and so can be made with glorious abandon. Even if you reach that fork in the road with enemies hot on your heels, you can still go the wrong way. If they catch up and casually separate your head from your shoulders, you'll just resurrect intact at a checkpoint a few minutes down the road. Try again. Real life is not quite so forgiving. Each of the million decisions made in a day nudges you into a different future. The accumulated weight of so many choices can become paralyzing, particularly in a society that demands we pursue total life optimization, dispatching every minute with brutal efficiency.

Perhaps there is something to be learned from the pathfinding of the gaming world. Games have always been ground zero for exploration, a space where play is taken seriously and experimentation is rigorously encouraged. They teach us that taking time for discovery yields unexpected rewards—moments of grace that you might miss if you're always hurtling faster toward goalposts that, on closer inspection, only ever move further away.

Granted, the spirit of risk-taking is not appropriate in every life situation. Some decisions require careful consideration and firm resolve. There is no button to reload and start again. So other digital landscapes may be more instructive here. Perhaps the alien planets beckoning interstellar explorers, which teach us that looking beyond our horizons can bring us closer to a human truth. Or the intricate games which lead players through vast desert environments using only the faintest cues. There we are encouraged to observe every detail of a situation before choosing a path of action, since it is the angle of the cresting dune or the shadow thrown by the lone eagle that subtly guides us home. The ceaseless surge of life is represented most simply in old-fashioned side-scrolling arcade games. In these, following the logic of reading, you can only move from left to right. Mario can jump into the clouds or dive to the depths of the sea, but he cannot turn around. He understands, as we do, that there is only ever one direction: forward.

Words by Tom Faber

GAME PLAN

by Tom Faber

Video games can teach us about real-world problems. In 2005, a glitchy update to the online fantasy game *World of Warcraft* caused "corrupted blood"—a contagious disease—to escape Hakkar the Soulflayer's dungeon home and spread across the virtual world. Low-level players in main cities were wiped out in minutes. Bustling marketplaces turned to ghost towns, carpeted with skeletons. Those who would normally cooperate quarantined themselves in remote locations. The incident attracted the interest of real-world epidemiologists, who used it as a case study of how humans respond to contagion. They discovered bravery in the healers and the unanticipated ghoulish curiosity of hundreds who approached the infected for a closer look.

Devendra Banhart

An interview with the soft-spoken pied piper of psychedelic Bohemia.

"Press the button of world peace and wipe out everything but the moon," Devendra Banhart sings on his new album, *Ma*. You would be forgiven for assuming that the current state of the planet has turned Banhart into a nihilist. Thankfully, he's just exasperated. At 38, the maniacally creative musician, poet and artist is still as inventive as ever; his 10th studio album brings together cheeky folk songs, winsome rock and even loping Japanese country-pop. Banhart says he "let the lyrical narrative lead the way," and *Ma* returns again and again to the unexpected (and even uninvited) consequences of love: romantic fervor, filial devotion and the love of one's homeland—Venezuela, in Banhart's case, and its disastrous ongoing political crisis.[1]

SM: *What's it like to talk to people about your art? Is it alienating? Helpful?*
DB: It's definitely the oddest part of my life. My work is about disappearing and observing—that's how material is accumulated and eventually becomes a song, poem or painting. Talking about myself is the complete opposite; at the same time, it's an amazing opportunity to talk about art and music that I find exciting and interesting, or to talk about issues that are important to me, like Venezuela.

SM: *Venezuela is clearly at the center of a lot of songs on* Ma, *but I wonder if you feel your music has always contained a political element. Is there any distinction for you between your earlier work and something like* Ma's *"Abre Las Manos"?* **DB:** I've [generally] felt that a gentle approach is more effective. It's just that, A: We've all been politicized by the amount of suffering and madness that's occupying so many global seats of power. And B: This particular moment is *so* apocalyptic for Venezuela. Having been there myself only two years ago and thinking it couldn't possibly get any worse than what I was seeing—then seeing it get a thousand times worse.

SM: *Like several of your other albums,* Ma *has snatches of songs in many different languages—English, Spanish, Japanese and Portuguese. When you're writing music, how do you choose which language to use?* **DB:** It's the gist of the song that determines the language in which it is sung. For example, there's a song on the album called "Carolina." It's about the song "Carolina" by Chico Buarque—which is in Portuguese. The thing is, I don't really speak Portuguese—so the song ends with me admitting that I should probably learn it. I suppose that could have worked much better in English, actually…

SM: *Seeing as you're well-traveled—as a person and as a musician— what's your secret to a successful voyage?* **DB:** It's hard to beat underwear and toiletries—and yet to this day, after a 15-hour flight, I often open up my suitcase and there's only one pair of underwear and no toothbrush. Last time I had 18 pairs of socks and two pairs of underwear, no deodorant but four shower caps. So the moral is: Don't pack drunk! I also meditate every day, at home or on the road—this is the one discipline I can't afford to skip, though of course it's the thing my mind wants me to skip the most.[2] And try to remember you are a tourist not [just] in this place, but in existence itself. Toothpaste and underwear; be disciplined but not rigid; try to respond and not react; and in the words of my good friend Isaiah Seret, "Remember that embarrassing yourself is good karma!"
Interview by Sean Michaels

NOTES

1. About four million Venezuelans have emigrated since 2014, when the death of Hugo Chavez created a political crisis that snowballed into shortages of basic food and medical supplies and an ongoing currency crisis; inflation hit a staggering 10 million percent in 2019.
—

2. Banhart is also a daily practitioner of "tonglin," which translates from Tibetan as "taking and sending." This unpleasant-sounding (but apparently very beneficial) practice involves visualizing yourself breathing the pain and suffering of others into your lungs, and breathing out healing energy.

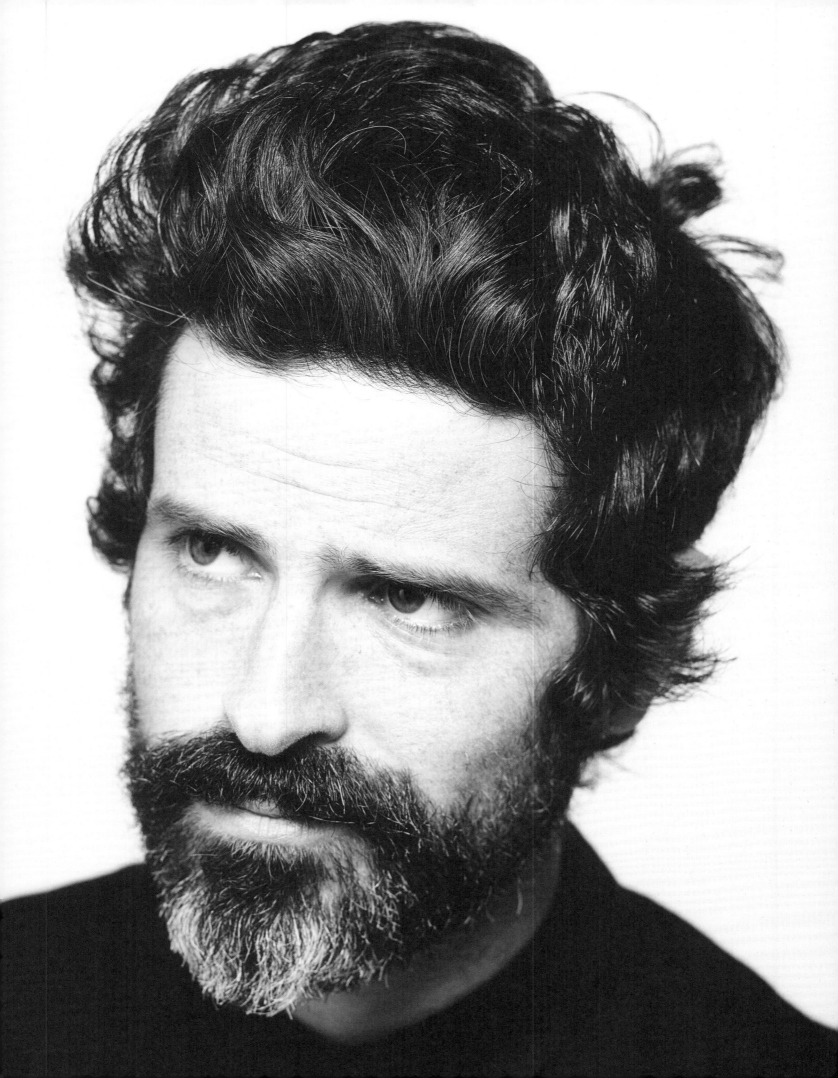

TO SEE THE SEA

by Tristan Rutherford

Railways created the British seaside resort during the Victorian era, offering millions their first ocean view. By "millions," read "the masses." The horsey set already had access to seaside escapes; it was the working classes who took advantage of the cheap vacations that trains provided, seeking respite from the dark satanic mills. Fish and chips and cotton candy unbuttoned Victorian morals, although track-drawn bathing cabins ensured that not an inch of thigh was shown when taking a dip. Airplanes sent the tide away. By delivering bargain packages that included flights, hotels and transfers, travel agents like Thomas Cook offered the British everyman his first glimpse of the Greek Islands or Spain's Costa del Sol. During the 1980s, accommodations back in Blackpool were boarded up or rented cheaply to the unemployed. Even as the tides receded, the seaside holiday remained engraved upon the British cultural memory, an ongoing source of fascination for documentary photographers such as Martin Parr. Has the tide turned again? A currency crash has enforced staycations for many Brits, while no-fly aspirations (not to mention the demise of Thomas Cook) also make a holiday at home look more appealing. Wooden piers now offer art galleries and *affogato* ice creams, along with the nostalgic memory of fried food and donkey rides. More than a century after their inception, the seaside resort has come of age. *Photograph: Romain Laprade / Aesop*

An open palm is a kind of paradox, isn't it? It's so inviting, so yielding: "Hands up," after all, is the international motion for surrender. But there's also a parallel universe of symbolism—a sense of mystery—hidden within that soft flesh. There can be an appeal to divinity in the open palm, a belief in a higher power. Look at all those saints in Christian art, their palms raised to the sky as they exhort God. The open palm can also be an act of violence, of interpersonal warfare—a slap across the cheek.[1] Or it can be an act of community—the handshake, two palms meeting each other in a gesture of goodwill.

As far as forms of divination go, palmistry might not be having quite the same renaissance as astrology or tarot, but it's probably even more accessible—we have a life line, a heart line, a head line; our entire futures mapped out right there. When Björk growls "Show me your palms" in one of her songs, what is she hoping to see? What can we read in our own lines or those of friends or lovers?

Imprinted in the palm is destiny or fate. The longer the life line, the more well-balanced the person, apparently. A longer heart line signifies openness and warmth. It may seem like a game, but each person's palmar creases are uniquely personal. Unlike wrinkles, which develop out of the inevitability of aging, palm lines are some of the few lines we're born with. We can grasp our fate: It's all right there, in the palm of our hands—if you know how to read it.[2]

Words by Rhian Sasseen

Show Your Hand

A short study of the palm.

NOTES

1. Hand gestures are so integral to human communication that there are now around 20 emojis featuring hands. The finger-and-thumb gesture, or Okay sign, was recently added to a list of hate symbols by the Anti-Defamation League due to its increased use by alt-right individuals as an underhand signal of white supremacy.

2. In palmistry, the fate line is believed to foretell circumstances beyond the individual's control. It runs from the bottom of the palm near the wrist, up through the center of the palm toward the middle finger.
—
—
—

Photograph: Mar + Vin, Styling: Maika Mano, Jewelry: Andrea Conti. Makeup: Lucas Lisboa

Photograph: Michael Oliver Love

The Long Short

On the mechanics of slow motion.

Nearly every film has one: a climactic scene in which everything around the hero slows down. There might be slow running, slow falling, or even the squint of slow recognition, each meant to signal a moment in which something is about to change. In *The Matrix*, which features one of the most famous slow-mo scenes in movie history, Keanu Reeves' Neo manipulates time to dodge a spray of bullets coming at him. Directors use this technique to heighten the emotion of what we're watching—to highlight what's important in no uncertain terms. Turns out, our brains do it, too.

In reality, when our brains sense danger—whether we're being shot at, darting after a child running into traffic, or falling off a cliff—time does not slow down, nor do we access a latent superpower to see it as such. Instead, it's how we *remember* what happened—should we survive it—that makes time lag. The brain's amygdala, which controls how we process emotions, simply codes more memories when we're in peril. It's that increased level of detail that affects our perception of how long something lasted: There's more to remember. This phenomenon is partly why time feels expansive when you're a child—so much is new that you can't help but take in the scenery.

Perhaps that's the trick to getting a grasp on that wily animal, time: Notice more. After all, you don't have to be pushed off a bridge to behold its many rivets and bolts. You don't have to be young to make new memories. You can start any time—even right now.

Words by Kyla Marshell

Power Down

On the pointlessness of power moves.

Power is a potent drug. It's why the language we use to describe it is laced with that of addiction. We crave it. Or we're power-hungry. Power-mad. Drunk on power. On a power trip.

A power move is like a quick fix down a back alley—a desperate hit for the vulnerable ego. A person comfortable in authority does not need to flaunt it, but those who are insecure about their position become giddy on assertions of their dominance.

We all know the drill: Someone makes you wait unreasonably long for a meeting to emphasize how valuable their time is; the boss insists on sitting at the head of the table; a parent undermines their offspring's partner to demonstrate an exclusive hold over their affections.[1]

For evidence that power moves are comfort blankets for the insecure, watch videos of Donald Trump engaging in desktop "manspreading"—rearranging other people's belongings on tables during meetings. It is petty, disconcerting and conspicuously bizarre.[2] Power moves work precisely because of this weirdness. In a recent *New Yorker* interview, illusionist Derren Brown describes his technique for hypnosis in these terms: "Induce confusion."

But power moves are arguably counterproductive. "It's bad leadership," says Liz Fosslien, co-author of *No Hard Feelings: The Secret Power of Embracing Emotions at Work.* "If you're constantly pulling power moves, you're wasting energy that could be used to solve problems." Moreover, she points out, they don't make for an environment in which people feel comfortable speaking up—it's far more effective to strip away conventional hierarchies, for example by going for a walk with a member of staff. Power moves, she says, can also trap you in your own tyranny: "You're going to have to keep pulling the power move to keep your authority, because the only thing keeping people in line is fear."

Power is, of course, distributed unequally across society—women and people of color, for example, must often find ways to grasp it. Although hardly among the downtrodden, Akie Abe, the Japanese prime minister's wife, found her own subtle way of handling the most powerful man in the world by reportedly pretending not to speak English for the entire duration of a meal sitting next to Trump.

Refusing to engage is perhaps the most effective counterweight to those who wield power recklessly. And watch out for patterns, know your own triggers, work out how to not be thrown by the power-hungry, and let them outmaneuver themselves. In Derren Brown's terms: Don't let them induce confusion.

Words by Debika Ray

Photograph: Charlotte Lapalus

NOTES

1. In *The 48 Laws of Power*, American author Robert Greene draws on the philosophies of Machiavelli, Sun Tzu and Carl von Clausewitz to distill a 3,000-year history of power into 48 self-help strategies to achieve total domination. Since publishing in 1998, it has turned Greene, as *The Los Angeles Times* noted, into a "cult hero with the hip-hop set, Hollywood elite and prison inmates alike."

2. Another overt power move favored by President Trump is his handshake, which has at times included yanking another off-balance (then-Supreme Court nominee Neil M. Gorsuch), ignoring the invitation completely (German Chancellor Angela Merkel), or else never letting go (famously, his 29-second handshake with French President Emmanuel Macron in 2017).

In Search of
the Lizard People

Behind the bent logic of conspiracists.

Depending on who you talk to, Paul McCartney is either alive and well or he was brutally decapitated in a car accident decades ago. In 1966, McCartney's decision to retreat from the public eye—coupled with a series of cryptic messages in The Beatles' music that fans claimed to decode—resulted in the theory that Paul was dead and the rest of the band was covering it up. Should you be wondering who has stood in for McCartney all these years, it's an orphaned Scottish look-alike named Billy Shears who was trained to impersonate him.

When a monumental event happens, there's usually a conspiracy theory to explain it. The mass shooting at Sandy Hook Elementary School was staged so that the US government could clamp down on guns; global warming is a hoax hatched by scientists; reptilian overlords masquerading as humans were responsible for the Holocaust. Psychological research into the popularity of such theories suggests that people are drawn to them as a way to preserve their belief systems in the face of rapid social change. Disenfranchisement, distressing feelings of uncertainty, and dissatisfaction with the mundane explanation attached to a large-scale and impactful event lead people to seek control in theories underpinned by negative and distrustful ideology.

The "Paul is dead" conspiracy bloomed in an environment ripe with suspicion and paranoia. President John F. Kennedy had been assassinated in what some believed was a coup. America's youth-led cultural revolution saw skepticism toward the mainstream media gain traction as the Vietnam War raged on. For Beatles fans, poring over song lyrics and album covers, it was easy to find subliminal messages that explained why the star had gone quiet. In a society upended by seismic changes, their feverish speculation fit within a broader malaise.

Even after McCartney appeared on the cover of *Life* magazine in 1969, accompanied by the headline "Paul is still with us," the rumors persisted. So if evidence won't persuade a conspiracy theorist, what will? Based on a study by Kellogg School of Management professor Cynthia Wang, the best approach is probably to change tack. Because people turn to false narratives as a coping mechanism for feelings of alienation and anxiety, Wang asked participants in her study to write about their ambitions instead. As their attention shifted from the abstract to the concrete, the propensity to grasp at outlandish explanations diminished. Encouraging an increased sense of control, it turns out, is the most effective intervention for a conspiracy theorist: The world feels less daunting when attention is focused on the parts of it that can be controlled.

Words by Pip Usher

2.

Features

---

42 — 112

Greta Lee built her reputation playing charismatic outsiders in other people's stories. Now, she's writing her own.

Words by *Rachel Syme*, Photography by *Dominik Tarabanski* & Styling by *Jordy Huinder*

Greta Lee did not want us to end up at Dimes. The tiny, cliquish café on the Lower East Side of Manhattan, with its pastel cafeteria tables and oversized palm fronds and pillowy tahini toasts, is such a *scene*, after all. It's the kind of place where you can find runway models and Swedish tourists alike sitting on the blond wood bar stools all day long, sipping orange blossom kefir and eating macrobiotic power bowls. It's not that Lee objects to any of this, really, it's just that she wanted to take me somewhere a little more *New York*.

Her first idea was to meet for breakfast at the nearby Golden Diner, a new greasy spoon that prides itself on being old school: The chef, Samuel Yoo, set out to replicate the classic Queens diners of his youth, chrome swivel stools and all. Lee worked with Yoo, once upon a time in the aughts, when she was a server at Momofuku Ko, David Chang's Michelin-starred restaurant where it is still impossible to get a reservation. She thought it might be poetic, to nod at how far they'd come since: Yoo with his own establishment, she the co-star of Netflix's *Russian Doll* who is also writing and producing her own comedy show for HBO.

But things do not go to plan. When I arrive at the diner on a chilly morning in late October, Lee is waiting outside, slumped against the locked front door with her arms crossed and a bemused look on her face. She is wearing high-waisted linen pants topped with an oversized ivory cardigan that ties together in the front with red ribbons (the sweater is from YanYan, a new independent label founded by the designers Phyllis Chan and Suzzie Chung out of a desire to update traditional Chinese clothing; Lee found them on Instagram). The outfit—along with her short black bob—makes her look simultaneously five and 95 years old. She later tells me that this is the exact aesthetic she is going for. Her style icons are babies and "old New Yorkers eating ice cream in the parks. If you see an octogenarian eating ice cream, chances are their outfit is what I want."

The diner, as it turned out, was closed on Mondays. "Oh well," Lee says, with sigh, "Dimes it is." After we sit down and order our green juices and Love Toast, she tells me that if she'd been hesitant to eat here, it was because it feels "very Los Angeles." Lee, who is 36, spent most of her youth in LA, but she moved away after high school and never wanted to return. When she was a teenager, growing up in La Cañada Flintridge, a tiny neighborhood wedged between Glendale and South Pasadena, she would drive up to the dusty parking lot of a local country club and look out over the city lights. While some might have found this view romantic, Lee felt disenchanted by what she saw. "I was really having that *Little Mermaid* moment," she says. "I wanted to get *out there*, far away. I think I was just one of those kids who, from a young age, really wanted to be in New York."

Lee did live in New York City as a small child, but she was too young to really remember it. Her parents, who met in Seoul, moved first to Los Angeles, where Lee was born in the early 1980s, but they quickly ended up bouncing around the country. Her father, a doctor, "couldn't find a hospital that would hire him because he didn't speak English," Lee says. The family moved to Springfield, Massachusetts, then Canarsie, Brooklyn (Lee has two younger siblings, one born in each city), and then eventually back to Los Angeles,

where they settled long-term. Telling me this story, Lee brings up the concept of sacrifices. Her mother, who was an accomplished classical pianist in South Korea, "moved here, and stopped," Lee says. "And she basically just took care of us until we left for college."

Because her mother abandoned her own artistic ambitions, Lee, who grew up singing and dancing, felt doubly driven to pursue a life as a performer. She studied musical theater at Northwestern University in Chicago (where she met her husband, the actor and writer Russ Armstrong) and then immediately moved to New York City, hoping to start her life as a professional actress.

Right away, Lee landed a role on *Law & Order: SVU* in an episode called "Taboo," in which she played the roommate of a girl embroiled in an incest scandal. Shortly after that, she was cast in the national touring production of the comic musical *The 25th Annual Putnam County Spelling Bee* as Marcy Park, a stressed-out, overachieving star student who only sleeps three hours a night. Lee opened the show in San Francisco, then Boston, and then moved back to

New York, where she stepped into the role on Broadway. By the time she was 25, Lee had performed thousands of times, to crowds all over the country. She thought she had it made.

"I thought I was going to become the Korean Natalie Portman of my generation," she says, with a laugh. "I was like, 'I've made it. Goodbye everyone!' I had no idea that after that show ended, it was like oh, now you go wait tables for many, many, years."

During her whirlwind of theatrical success, Lee would regularly buy drinks for all her friends with her measly Broadway salary ("Some of them were *bankers*. What the fuck was I thinking?") and racked up more credit card debt than she'd like to admit trying to emulate the extravagant New York fantasy she had in her head when she was a child. "I was an asshole trying to be Carrie Bradshaw," she jokes. "I got here and just threw away money... I think I would have a house if it weren't for *Sex and the City*."

When *Spelling Bee* closed in 2008, Lee found herself suddenly out of work and unable to find it again. The role of Marcy—a meaty,

"I waited tables on a lot of people I've worked with since."

Left: Lee wears a dress by Moon Choi and mules by Christian Wijnants. Chair: LC8 by Charlotte Perriand from Cassina. Right: Lee wears a dress by COS and boots by Christian Wijnants. Chair: LC9 by Charlotte Perriand from Cassina. All earrings by A.P.C.

Set Design: Javier Irigoyen, Hair: Eloise Cheung, Makeup: Rommy Najor.

scenery-chewing part for an Asian woman—turned out to be more of an exception than the rule. Lee started hostessing at the buzzy Momofuku Ssäm Bar, and then graduated to "senior server," helping to open other David Chang restaurants, including Ko and Má Pêche. She was determined to keep auditioning, but she also became more and more entrenched in the food world. "It's hard for me to do something casually. I definitely got sucked in," she says. "I waited tables on a lot of people I've worked with since, and it's a kind of a private joke that I have. Because they don't remember, but I'm like, *I have served you pork buns, sir.*"

In 2012, Lee took a small part in *4000 Miles*, a Pulitzer finalist play by Amy Herzog that premiered at Lincoln Center. She almost said no, because her character was only in one scene. She played Amanda, a Chinese woman who is dating the lead actor, who has returned to New York City to visit his surly grandmother. Her presence is meant to provoke the old woman, to serve as a visual shock. "It's this big, explosive moment, storywise," Lee says, "But that's actually one of my gripes about contemporary American theater. I felt like the parts for minorities, in this world of, like, *prestige* family drama plays... If I'm gonna be in it, I'm going to be, like, fucking the son. It's like the outsider can only be invited in in a very specific way."

Her one scene did make a big impression—namely on a young Lena Dunham. After seeing Lee in the play, Dunham wrote her into *Girls* as the snotty gallerina, Soojin. Then, at a table read for *Girls*, Lee reconnected with the comedian Amy Schumer, who she'd first met in an elevator after an audition. Schumer cast Lee in her Comedy Central show *Inside Amy Schumer* (you may remember seeing Lee in that viral

"Compliments" sketch, in which a group of women put themselves down to the point of violent absurdity). Around the same time, Lee appeared in a web episode of the show *High Maintenance*, which has since transferred to HBO, as "Homeless Heidi," a woman who squats in a Tinder flame's apartment because she doesn't have a place to live. In 2014, Lee played a similar role on *New Girl* as Jake Johnson's love interest Kai, who he thinks is also a grifter until she reveals she is secretly an heiress.

While Lee suddenly started to land parts—and thanks to her droll, deadpan affect stood out whenever she was on screen—the fact that her success was mediated through a series of white women creators began to grind away at her. "Even with my closest peers, I will have a moment of realizing, 'Oh. You still see the world that way,'" she says, taking a bite of scrambled eggs. "Like I can only be part of this story as a complete outsider. Basically the racism is so systemic, and we're not close to fixing that."

One day, when Lee was griping to Schumer about the lack of hefty material for Asian women, Schumer told her that the only solution was for Lee to write it herself. "She was sort of like, 'Okay dummy, so just open up your laptop and go tap-tap-tap and and write it,'" Lee says. "Which is also very funny, 'cause it's not, obviously, that easy." Lee sat down to write, but felt angry about having to do it in the first place. "I felt genuinely upset that in order for me to keep doing what I had envisioned, I would have to take on this other arm," she says. "I was coming to terms with really seeing just how much I was not represented. At all. It's still a hard pill to swallow. And to keep waking up to the same world."

At first, Lee says, the scripts she wrote were "a lot of goo, honestly just terrible." But over time she gained confidence, and along with her friend Jason Kim, who was a story editor on *Girls* and is currently a producer for the HBO show *Barry*, began to build a show around a scheming Korean

Lee wears a suit by Eckhaus Latta and mules by Christian Wijnants. Chair: LC1 by Le Corbusier, Pierre Jeanneret and Charlotte Perriand from Cassina.

woman in Los Angeles who has expensive taste and may or may not be committing crimes to fuel her desires. "She's almost like the most whitewashed version of myself," Lee says. "Like if I lived in Brentwood. And if I was modeling myself off a Barbie doll."

They called the show *Koreatown*, and pitched it to HBO in 2018. The network bought the idea right away. It has taken some time for Lee and Kim to get the process moving—she just turned in the final scripts a few days before we met—but she is confident that it will be made. She is writing the show she always wanted to see, about a complicated Asian family—one that's sometimes on the wrong side of the law. When she compared the show to *The Sopranos* in interviews after it sold, she received some criticism from those who were worried that she would portray the Korean community in a negative light. And this is the crux of the problem, she says; there are so few shows that feature minorities that creators feel an extra burden to write feel-good stories. But Lee believes that she—and her characters—should be able to be as wicked and sardonic and morally complex as anybody else.

"People said, 'Ooh but is that going to make Koreans look bad, like are you going to make them criminals?'" she says. "I mean that was really surprising because I thought, no one's watching *The Sopranos* and saying 'Oh no. We're going to make Italians look bad!' There is such a double standard."

Once Lee started writing her own material, she found it difficult to stop. Now, in addition to *Koreatown*, she is working on two other projects, both feature films about Korean women. One is a farcical sitcom imagining the life of Kim Jong Un's sister. "There's this conspiracy theory that his right-

"The trick of being a 'modern woman' is 'You have the privilege to be stretched incredibly thin.'"

hand man is actually his sister," Lee says. "And, I just thought, there's something so fun about 'Okay, how do we push this female empowerment all the way to arrive at where women too can become sociopathic?'"

Her other project is a more serious endeavor. She is trying to write the story of the Kim Sisters, a Korean singing trio during the 1950s and '60s who started entertaining GIs during the Korean War and then went on an incredibly successful tour of the United States. "They are, I think, the first, K-pop group historically," Lee says. "They came over to the States to perform on *The Ed Sullivan Show*."

The fact that the Kims' story has been lost to time, even though they performed for Ed Sullivan 21 times, is an act of erasure that Lee feels very motivated to correct. "These women, first of all, are amazing," she says. "They learned, I think, 20 instruments each. They're musical prodigies. They had to learn English to survive... And no one knows who they are."

While Lee is working behind the scenes to address historical invisibility, she is becoming more and more visible in front of the camera. She appeared recently in Leslye Headland's cult hit *Russian Doll* as a bohemian friend throwing Natasha Lyonne a birthday party (over, and over and over). Because of the cyclical conceit of the show, viewers hear Lee coo the line "Sweet Birthday Baby!" at the top of almost every episode. Now, people regularly bark the line at her on the street.

"That's a new thing," she says, as we finish our last bites of toast slathered in tahini and berry jam. "I feel like I've been doing this for a long time, but I've never had a catchphrase."

While Lee feels more or less indifferent about becoming a meme, she says her three-year-old son, Apollo, gets a kick out of it. "He's a very exuberant chatty fellow," she says. "And he likes to point out all the time that it's not Mommy's birthday." Apollo is big brother to Raphael, who was born just last year.

At the moment, Lee's life feels like a delicate balancing act. She's trying to juggle a family (she's one of the only people she knows with two kids under five), a New York apartment (she still doesn't want to move back to LA, though she realizes it's probably inevitable), an acting career (she'll be in *Russian Doll*'s top-secret second season) and the chance to shepherd to the screen the sort of stories she never saw growing up. "I think that the trick of being a 'modern woman' is like 'You have the privilege to be stretched incredibly thin,'" she says, slurping down a second cup of coffee.

After we meet, Lee has to run to Brooklyn to go to couples therapy with her husband (they are doing great, they just go for maintenance), then pick up Apollo and Raphael ("my children for better or for worse are undeniably 98% of my existence right now"), then go over *Koreatown* scripts, then prepare to fly to Europe to film a new television show that she can't yet discuss. It's a jampacked life, but she is far happier having too much work to do than she was serving ramen, daydreaming about someone writing a good part for her. One day, she simply got angry enough, and tired enough of waiting around, to write her own dream role. And now, she'll be able to create similar opportunities for other women like herself. She no longer needs to fantasize about becoming the Korean Natalie Portman of her generation; she's her generation's one and only Greta Lee.

Essay:

Can't Hack It Anymore

Words by Hettie O'Brien

If you can hack a computer's software, can you hack a person's life? During the first part of the 21st century, a wave of optimistic tech geeks thought so, proclaiming that the way to increase productivity—from sleeping efficiently to removing household stains—was to find and exploit shortcuts in the way we "code" daily life. Hettie O'Brien charts the rise and eventual mutation of an early internet philosophy.

Wake up. Make your bed before drinking a cup of "titanium tea" mixed from two varieties of tea, a tablespoon of coconut oil, grass-fed butter and a pinch of turmeric. Meditate for 20 minutes, followed by a two-minute decompression period. Complete 20 minutes of light exercise and spend five minutes committing your thoughts to the pages of a journal. You are now ready—finally— to begin the day. This may all sound excessive, but these instructions form the morning routine of a prominent member of the "life hacking" community, whose net worth is reportedly $100 million, and who claims his most productive working hours are between 1 a.m. and 4 a.m.

For some, the challenge of being constantly productive in an increasingly demanding world is akin to rewriting a piece of software to make it run more reliably. And just as computer programmers learn the rules of a system and then exploit "hacks" to subvert its mainframe, the emergence of a movement of life hackers in the early 21st century applied the same approach to life off-screen. Life hackers see the world as a system with two sets of rules: the rules that everyone else follows, and the *real* rules. Hackers believe that they are able to discern this underlying set of rules and exploit them for their own ends, short-circuiting a switchboard to simplify the route from A to B. Computer programmers might use techniques to manage projects at work; life hackers bring them home. If every generation gets the self-help philosophy it deserves, life hacking reflects a world where work exceeds the boundaries of a nine-to-five schedule and many of us submit to being captured, optimized and appropriated by technology platforms.

The recent history of life hacking dates back to 2004, when the writer Danny O'Brien introduced the term in a presentation at the O'Reilly Emerging Technology Conference in San Diego. O'Brien sent questionnaires to numerous "over-prolific alpha geeks," asking how they managed to accomplish so much while avoiding technological distraction. His contention was that these pointy-heads had found strategies for working effectively in an endlessly distracting world. Fifteen years later, the term has evolved in a more banal direction. Googling "life hacks" today pulls up an array of mundane (and occasionally revelatory) domestic tips, including removing toilet stains with Coca-Cola, waterproofing shoes with a layer of beeswax and rubbing your skin with oranges to neutralize the smell of sweat.[1]

The heyday of life hacking was in the early years of this century, when people were still enamored with technology and "disruption" was seen in a purely positive light. Computer programmers and "tech bros" were the new prophets of this digital age, famed for their alleged genius, ferocious work ethic and ability to reap boundless fortunes. Many of the original exponents of life hacking now eschew the term: Some turned to new trends like "digital minimalism," an ethos that involves zealously decluttering your life, Marie Kondo–style, while others dropped out of the life hacking scene altogether, denouncing its obsession with productivity.[2] Although we no longer look to Silicon Valley as a beacon of self-help, the idea that life could be approached like an operating system still endures today—and reflects our troubling passion for extracting productivity from every waking moment.

"Self-help, when you look at its history, reoccurs every 10, 20 or 30 years. Every new generation that appears in the workplace is like, 'Okay, how do I find my way—and what do I do?'" Joseph Reagle, an associate professor of communication studies at Northeastern University and author of a brief history of the life-hacking movement, *Hacking Life*, tells me.

One of the most significant effects of having workplace managers in the 20th century was the dramatic increase in the productivity of manual workers. But what happens when you're your own manager—when work no longer takes place in the office, and the office can be a bed or coffee shop? For many professionals and freelancers with varying degrees of security, the boundary between work and leisure is increasingly porous: They can make money during every waking moment, and they spend their free time promoting their personal brand on social media. Time becomes a prized resource, and productivity is a way of measuring value.

Though Reagle thinks life hacking can be a helpful tool, he admits that it has limitations: "You're inherently blocking out the periphery underfoot, and you might not be appreciating the bigger picture, the system you're in, the people you're elbowing aside," he says.

Indeed, the results of this mindset can be darker than they first appear. Take an example that was widely reported by news outlets in 2013: "Bob"—an employee of US telecom company Verizon, outsourced his job as a computer programmer to a worker in the Chinese city of Shenyang. Bob paid the worker one-fifth of his six-figure salary, and over several years received excellent performance reviews for his "clean, well written" coding (he was also named "the best developer in the building," according to Verizon). While at work, Bob spent hours surfing Reddit, watching cat videos on YouTube and chatting with people on Facebook. Was this a "hack"—or an exploitative lie that exposed the kinks in our economy?

Outsourcing is common among committed life hackers, and many don't see a problem with contracting underpaid workers to do the tasks they don't have the time to undertake. For instance, Maneesh Sethi, a self-proclaimed life hacker and founder of a wearables company, reportedly paid a Filipino worker

---

NOTES

1. Questionable life hacks that did the rounds in the early aughts include the following: Using tea bags as hand warmers; using a fork as a spoon by covering it in tape; freezing slivers of toothpaste to serve as after-dinner mints; using sanitary pads as hip padding.

2. All lifestyle trends have their own lifespan. In late 2019, after a decade of counseling people to declutter their houses, Japanese tidying guru Marie Kondo surprised devotees when she opened an online store selling ornamental computer cleaning brushes and flower bouquet tote bags.

to remind him to floss. If life hacking is a "philosophy," the idea of outsourcing tasks to the gig economy seems a far cry from the mantra that we should treat others as we ourselves would like to be treated.

Life hacking is "kind of like horse blinkers," Reagle says. This analogy was brought to life by Japanese tech giant Toshiba, which prototyped a set of noise-canceling blinkers that it previewed last year at South by Southwest, an annual festival in Texas popular with tech employees. "You could put this cubicle on your head while your spouse was playing with your kid in order to focus on your work. I just found it deliciously ironic," Reagle adds.

Blinkering ourselves to the world can distract us from what matters. As the writer and artist Jenny Odell describes in her book, *How to Do Nothing*, resisting the constant lure of productivity leads to more meaningful understandings of happiness and political engagement. Rather than recommending a digital detox retreat or mindfulness course, though, Odell sees "doing nothing" as "an active process of listening" and focusing our attention on the details of our environment. She likens this rejection of productivity to bird-watching, or being out in nature and focusing one's gaze deeply on the minute changes in a landscape. "What amazed and humbled me about bird-watching was the way it changed the granularity of my perception, which had been pretty 'low-res,'" she writes. The effects of this change in perception can be profound. "When the pattern of your attention has changed, you render your reality differently. You begin to move and act in a different kind of world."

"Life hackers see the world as a system with two sets of rules: the rules that everyone else follows, and the real rules."

Life hacking reflects an obsession with making every moment productive. But philosophers have long argued that unproductive time is an important part of being human. The German thinker Friedrich Schiller thought what he called the "play drive" was intrinsic to human creativity. "If you have a domain that is separated from the normal demands of everyday life, and it's meant to be inconsequential—in the sense that there aren't heavy penalties or consequences—that is precisely something that can liberate creative thinking," John Tasioulas, a professor of philosophy at King's College London who has written on the importance of play, tells me.

Tasioulas argues that our productivity-fixated society risks occluding the importance of leisure and play—things that should exist for their own sake. "We're not just material beings constantly engaged in economic activity; there has to be space for something else... another kind of value, which threatens to be crowded out if we're constantly in a productive, economic, work-focused mode." In an era when our attention is the most valuable and overspent resource, resisting the siren call of productivity may prove far more radical than any hack.

LES JARDINS DE MARQUEYSSAC

In these maze-like gardens, getting lost turns out to be the most sensible path to take. Photography by Romain Laprade @ Styling by Camille-Joséphine Teisseire

Planted relentlessly during the 1860s, there are over 150,000 topiaried boxwoods at the Jardins de Marqueyssac.

Below: Kaissan wears a turtleneck by De Fursac. Right: He wears a suit by Alexander McQueen.

Below: Kaissan wears a jacket by Hermès and shorts by Lacoste.

Left: Kaissan wears a turtleneck by De Fursac and trousers and a belt by Dior Men. Above: He wears a suit by Alexander McQueen.

Kaissan wears a jacket by Wales Bonner and a shirt by De Fursac.

MARYAM

Don't listen to the fans who call her "cool." The leader of New York's most admired fashion set is just a cuddlebug who really, really likes her friends. Words by Laura Rysman & Photography by Claire Cottrell

70

"I'm a cuddlebug. I can be into things that are very uncool."

"Welcome." Maryam Nassirzadeh bestows her greeting upon me in a conspiratorially low voice. Although we are not in her Lower East Side mecca of a store, but in a mostly empty and softly lit Italian café near her home in New York's NoHo neighborhood, it's clear that Nassirzadeh is accustomed to making everywhere she goes into her own domain. Seated at the dining room's first marble table, illuminated by the glow of the café's cheese counter, this popularly anointed oracle of downtown fashion is dressed for morning tea in an eloquent assembly of unlikely elements. She wears a Charvet button-down in thin blue pinstripes and a rainslicker-shiny patent skirt from her own line, paired with Margiela's iconically weird split-toe Tabi boots. Her broad eyebrows and long flaps of dark hair delineate her face, left natural except for a mauve swipe of lipstick. Nassirzadeh, 41, is unvarnished and eccentric, nonchalant and sophisticated. I would like to dress like her. Lots of people would like to dress like her.

Nassirzadeh has become a style heartthrob, a guru of what New York dressing looks like today, projecting her personal preferences through the cult Norfolk Street multi-brand boutique she opened in 2008, the wholesale showroom she added a year later and the celebrated clothing and accessories line she launched in 2012. Each one bears her full name. The shop—a platform for other arty designers which marked the beginning of her success—reverberated with a certain stylishly unconventional New Yorker: Its gallery-like atmosphere introduced a lifestyle of exotic travel and raw street photography and most of all, Nassirzadeh's highly curated, highly original conception of fashion.

"I know what works because my head is in design," she says, propping up her vintage Chanel PVC tote on the neighboring chair. She chooses brands not just for what she wears herself, but what attracts her, and who attracts her. "I want to discover and share someone's talent, and when you believe in something and fall for a designer's work, the integrity is there." She became an early champion of brands like Telfar and Eckhaus Latta—pioneering vanguard designers today crowned as leading icons of New York fashion.

Nassirzadeh describes each of her designers with passion, gushing over Veja's swoon-inducing drawings, or the poetic world of Cristaseya or

"I get very excited by people whose character comes out in every aspect of their self-expression."

the kindred spirit of Dumitrascu. Lauren Manoogian, Medea and Super Yaya all elicit giddy raves. She uses both hands to form their clothes and bags in the air between us. "There's something in these designers that took me back to part of myself and my own way of designing," she says. She admits to being surprised that her idiosyncratic outlook found so many devotees: "With the boutique, I was just expressing my taste and what I relate to, but it resonated with people."

Born in Iran and raised in California's San Fernando Valley, Nassirzadeh studied at the Rhode Island School of Design and then launched her first brand in Los Angeles—a line of hand-embellished T-shirts inspired by the experiments of her textile studies.[1] The collection sold at top stores including Barneys but, still in her early 20s, Nassirzadeh was overwhelmed by simultaneously designing and managing a business, and shuttered it to hone her ideas.

In 2006, Nassirzadeh arrived in New York for an intensive fashion course at Parsons School of Design. Three years later she founded the Maryam Nassir Zadeh store with Uday Kak, who became her husband and the father of her two children—aged nine and seven. It was a leap of faith back into fashion; Nassirzadeh felt that she couldn't start another clothing line after her first one petered out.

Designing your own line means creating "your ideal world, and I was really scared to try again, but I started feeling jealous of my designers," Nassirzadeh says, sipping from her porcelain teacup. After four successful years running the boutique, with a considerable audience already sold on her aesthetic wisdom, she inaugurated her new Maryam Nassir Zadeh line. Her minimal, retro-inspired shoes were a nearly instant and ubiquitous hit, and her runway shows are a highlight of New York Fashion Week. She sat out the February shows this year, though, to see if her designs "will be better without that pressure of putting on a show."

After years of building up a clientele, have her designs changed to suit its appetites? "Zero," she declares. "It's all about how I want to dress, about things I can't find, or something in my closet I'd like to do a different way—like a straw bag from Ibiza, my dad's shirt from the '80s, a Celine boot—and then people are drawn to what works for them in the collection." At her most recent show, an affair held on the asphalt of a Lower East Side park, bikini tops in place of shirts were paired with cargo pants and parachute-like skirts; miniskirts were too short to sit down in; lace layers peaked out from under sea-flower printed ensembles and jumpsuits. It was outlandish and personal, a mix-and-match pageant of unexpected proportions and private inspirations.

NOTES

1. Nassirzadeh's parents left Iran at the beginning of the revolution. In the 1970s, her grandmother owned a fashion-forward boutique in Tehran and her early influence honed Nassirzadeh's eye for interesting design.

2. Full moon gatherings are just one of the ways in which Nassirzadeh infuses her routine with a certain spiritualism. She attends twice-weekly Buddhist chanting sessions and refers to her running route along the East River as her "sacred ground."

Nassirzadeh will often work from her Manhattan apartment, pictured above.

"Having a store hasn't influenced my designing. It's only given me the confidence to really trust my own taste," Nassirzadeh says. "I'm just a warm and loving person that loves to celebrate people. I'm a cuddlebug. I can be into things that are very uncool. So I hate that cool factor attitude." To Nassirzadeh, cool implies a chimerical and even cynical embrace of trends, rather than the expression of the sincere emotions and imaginative individuality that drive her style. Then again, isn't true cool the heartfelt selfhood that's the opposite of trying?

"There are just times that you have an instinct and it clicks," she says about her choices, leaning in as the buzzing chatter of the early lunch crowd starts to compete with her hushed timbre. "When we first opened the store and we had the concept of lifestyle with curated objects and a variety of designers, I feel like that became a movement. The way my husband was photographing things in the sunlight, on the street—that's been a movement. The shoes, they had their movement too." Nassirzadeh's free-spirited intuition remains intact from her exploratory RISD days and her first attempts at a clothing line. But she's turned it into the flourishing business of store, showroom and clothing line—with a more clear-eyed approach, more focused on bolstering designers like herself, and with the support network of a like-minded team that works alongside her.

The store, where she occasionally hosts full moon all-night presentations accompanied by the music of a gong, has become a hub not just for the designers she champions, but also for an influential group of women, whose friendship with Nassirzadeh and affinity for her fashion choices have rendered them informal brand ambassadors.[2] She is the vibrant ringleader of this social circle, and a self-declared "connector" of people. (Midway through our conversation, she declares she must introduce me to friends of hers in Italy, where I'm based.)

"Women excite me," Nassirzadeh says, leaning in further across the table. "I get very excited by people whose character comes out in every aspect of their self-expression." Her friends, each an influencer in her own sphere and capturing, according to Nassirzadeh, a uniquely authentic style, all earn glowing descriptions: The artist Ana Kras, "love at first sight"; Daphne Javitch, a former underwear designer turned health mentor, "my lifestyle inspiration"; the jewelry designer Sophie Buhai, "total crush"; and Susan Cianciolo, a clothing artist whose crafty, freewheeling approach chimes with Nassirzadeh's own, "obsessed since forever." Ranging in age from 35 to 50, these women model for Nassirzadeh, incorporate her clothes into their wardrobes, and represent "character, personality and their unique way of being themselves. And they're so beautiful," she sighs. At the center of this entourage is Nassirzadeh herself, with her very personally inspired fashion and cadre of designers—uniting friends and captivating an eager public with her invitation not to dress like her in the end, but to dress like their more radical and unfettered selves.

"I was really scared to try again, but I started feeling jealous of my designers."

MNZ is Nassirzadeh's own line of clothing, accessories and shoes, which includes the Enzo purse, Cleo Slide and Palma High Sandal, pictured left.

SOFT STROKES

Fashion often looks to art for inspiration, so why not the other way round? Oil paintings by Diane Dal-Pra @ Styling by Tania Rat-Patron

Above: Skirt and sheer top by Max Mara. Right: Gown by Valentino and ring by Charlotte Chesnais.

A short stroll—and several wardrobe changes—with a woman who's never tired of New York. Words by Djassi DaCosta Johnson & Photography by *Andre D. Wagner*

Real estate agents rarely appear in the fashion pages of glossy magazines, but Lana Turner has never been much interested in doing what's expected of her. The Harlem local (and, many would say, legend) first caught the gaze of the fashion media thanks to her impeccable style—simultaneously classic and unusual—which has now been admired and photographed by several generations of New Yorkers. She once sold a hard-to-shift townhouse by mounting a display of her outfits inside it.

Turner is embedded in the history of Harlem—not just in its buildings, but also in its culture. I met her while working on programming with the literary society she's helmed for 38 years. She's currently organizing a season based around the life of Alain Locke, the philosopher, educator and "father" of the Harlem Renaissance. It's not so much that Turner is "more than" her style (500 boxed hats included), it's that she sees her wardrobe as integral to her entire outlook on life. Through her love of music, art, literature and—above all—New York City, Turner remains a perpetual student in her 70th year.

DDJ: *You began getting noticed because of how elegant your everyday wear is—equivalent to most Harlemites' "Sunday church" finery. Do you see personal style as a sort of public performance?* **LT:** We're oftentimes thinking about performance as something you get ready for—that you rehearse for, that you get costumed for, that you're directed for. Then there are those of us who have a life where the performance is all of the life. Even though I may pass through the world of the public during the course of a day, [dressing] starts out just for me. It starts out with "What is the weather?" "What is the sunshine?" "What are the clouds?" I really think about all that, and it colors what I choose to adorn myself with. How I am presenting myself to the world is not necessarily always for the world of eyes. Because, well, how do the birds present themselves? How did the tree leaves present themselves? How do the squirrels and the chipmunks and the sparrows present themselves? They present themselves as their own performance. It's the way they're constructed—it's their DNA. And I think it's the same thing for me.

DDJ: *Can you pinpoint where your style outlook comes from?* **LT:** Most people imagine that it would be my mother or my aunts. It's really my father. I think of him as someone who always was "dressed"— dark pants, white shirt, a tie and wingtip shoes. [My love of] jazz also comes straight from my father because this is what he listened to. [George] Gershwin is what my father gave me. Cole Porter. He didn't discuss it, he just simply had it on the radio. I could hear the grandeur of New York in Gershwin. It was the music and it was the buildings. It was the architecture and it was the light.

DDJ: *Do you enjoy the attention you get from admirers?* **LT:** You know, if you're walking down the street and someone pays you attention in New York City for no reason except that you have done something to distract their eyeballs for more than two seconds from their phones—you have actually done something! They may be appreciating you, but you're also loving them. I mean, it's easier to smile. It's easier to take in the beauty of what you see. When there is a response—not all people respond—they are usually giving you the best of themselves.

DDJ: *Are you as interested in New York as New York is in you?* **LT:** Walking is something that I love because living in New York City, there is always something going on in the street! I want to know, "Well, what is it?" "What has the culture done today?" I am a student of black culture. I've always known that black people perform when they step outside the door. Every day, there is somebody stepping outside totally unconcerned about whatever is happening next door. That they have their own and complete world that they're enmeshed in, and it's beautiful! There's a humor in it.

Turner says she always paid attention to the way she dressed, but for a long time didn't understand it as performance: "I came to it late in the knowing, but not in the doing," she explains.

"*There are those of us who have a life where the performance is all of the life.*"

The scale of Turner's fashion collection necessitated some innovative storage solutions: She hung white curtains along several walls of her Harlem home so that the space behind could be used for hanging clothes.

DDJ: *You've spent four decades at the helm of a Harlem literary society. What role has it played in your life?* **LT:** What is consistent is my intellectual side. There was always some place in my head that I made room for books, for ideas, for how to be. We're sitting in a room that is wall-to-wall books. My life is built on them. These days I'm steeped in my literary society and the world of Alain Locke through [Jeffrey C. Stewart's biography] *The New Negro*, and exploring Locke's emphasis on beauty and individuality in encouraging the African-American artists of the time to embrace their capacity for re-invention through African forms. I see that New Negro all over Harlem now.

DDJ: *How do you stay so curious?* **LT:** I work at understanding the world. And there's so much to "get" that I'm constantly aware of how much I don't know and how much I really want to know. That's where I end. I mean all of the other stuff is nice, but I constantly try to figure out, "How should I look at that painting?" or, "Why is that photograph relevant?"

DDJ: *Tell me about your love of dance.* **LT:** I'm not necessarily what I call a "showcase" dancer: I'm not the dancer that says to the audience, "I want you to look at me." My consciousness is really on my partner and what I'm hearing. Dancing with a partner is always wonderful. All that private insight, it's all happening, right there in front of a full audience. It's about the music for me. The dancing is part of it but the music is where I really come from. And it just makes you instinctively want to be a part of it.

DDJ: *You turned 70 this year. How would you rate your life satisfaction?* **LT:** I used to think that all the "extra" things I did were just that —they were extra. I never thought of them as being specific to who I am, largely because we're—at least in a Western culture anyway—demarcating our time by what we do for work. I would not have called myself an artist most of my life.

When you are just yourself—if you could just try and figure out where your *self* is—all the other things fall into place. And if you're giving the best of yourself, then you want to continue to move and improve on that. It leaves one with, "How can I make myself better?" There are so many things that go into that. But joy is at the top of it.

Turner was both a muse and friend of *New York Times* photographer Bill Cunningham, who chronicled fashion for the paper in his columns "On the Street" and "Evening Hour."

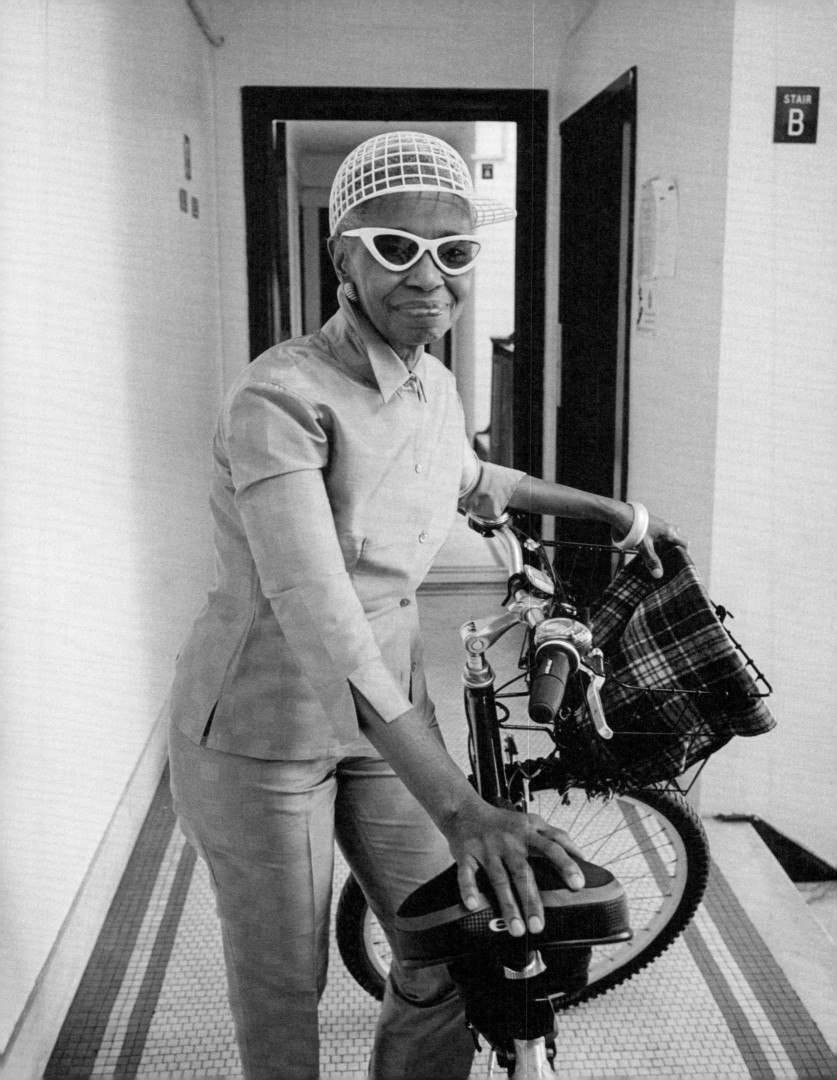

Home Tour:
Stephan Janson

How did an avowedly minimalist designer wind up as guardian of a Milanese temple to maximalism?

Words by *Laura Rysman*
Photography by *Christian Møller Andersen*

When Stephan Janson opens the door to the densely saturated *wunder-kammer* that is his Milan home, the only sensible response is to gasp. A taxidermied alligator stares stiffly at you, mounted on a 17th-century gilt wood settee of ripped silk, bought for a pittance from an antiques market. A full-wall vitrine encloses a riot of feathers: African and Amazonian headdresses, Native American war bonnets, Chinese hairpieces. Floor-to-ceiling shelves of books—part of the apartment's 25-year-old redesign by Roberto Peregalli—line every available wall, organizing the more than 20,000 volumes by art, history and other subjects. Hand-knotted carpets conceal the wooden floors, decorate walls as fragments in frames and even hang on curtain rods, shrouding the space in near darkness and blocking the chill from the windows in this mid-19th-century apartment, which lacks heating in several rooms. "Carpets on carpets on carpets," says Janson. "That's what this place is."

Insulated by the walls of books and layers of rugs, the warren of rooms teems with collections of superannuated beauties—Ancient Roman statuary, West African Nok sculptures from over 2,000 years ago, a 19th-century Alpine armoire encrusted with neat lines of woody pinecone scales. But Janson, a 62-year-old French fashion designer and couturier of bright frocks that defy trends, insists that all of this enchantment has nothing to do with him.

"I would live in a monk's cell if I could choose," he says, reclining on a velvet jacquard fauteuil against rows of books hung with small paintings on each shelf. "At 18, I painted my first apartment all white, and lived very happily in that kind of bare environment, until this place." This place—with its fading frescoed patterns on the walls and ceilings—is the work of Umberto Pasti, the man Janson has called his "consort" for the last 38 years, whom he met on a trip to Italy through a pair of twins. (In a meet-cute worthy of Shakespeare, Pasti had a fling with one of the brothers, and Janson with the other, yet the twins both realized their lovers were destined for each other and introduced them.)

Pasti is a writer, a garden designer and a fervent and encyclopedically informed antiquarian. ("Umberto," Janson confides, "comes from the kind of family where he's never really needed to work to support himself.") He began turning the five rooms of this apartment into his personal museum when the couple moved in 35 years ago, and continues to add treasures as he finds them, but he no longer lives here. The couple owns a property in the Moroccan countryside south of Tangier, where they replanted multitudes of bulbs uprooted by Tangier's urban development.

Janson worked with Diane von Furstenberg for several years, including on her New York boutique Diane. In her memoir she refers to him as a "talented young Frenchman" who she brought over from Italy.

Pasti's garden passions, previously limited to a shady patch outside of Janson's Milan atelier, became as absorbing as his love for antiques, and 20 years ago, he relocated to their seaside Tangier home to oversee the estate full-time. He has since become an international garden designer, and just published a book with Rizzoli, *Eden Revisited: A Garden in Northern Morocco*, that details the splendors of the Tangier project, beginning with a photo of the waist-high native iris species that now cover their house's hill in deep blues all the way down to the cobalt sea.

"I told him to move there," says Janson of the long distance. "It keeps the desire alive." So now Janson, a slender and boyish man with salt-and-pepper hair set off by heavy-framed dark glasses, lives surrounded by relics that are mostly not his own. "I don't like the idea of collecting at all," he says, relocating to a table covered by a threadbare 17th-century Turkish rug of faded turquoise and vermilion. "Umberto is a scholar, and I'm happy he's obsessed. I really enjoy it too, but I never would have chosen it."

A few of Janson's own possessions do dot the home's collections: scarabs in a narrow pair of vitrine boxes; a bronze lamp with a coiling snake gripping the lampshade, which was originally a gift from the poet Gabriele D'Annunzio to the actress Eleonora Duse; a portrait painted by Christian Bérard of the journalist Marie-Louise Bousquet, who introduced Pierre Bergé to Yves Saint Laurent—a present from his mother when he was 18, and already long-obsessed with the designer whose work inspired him to pursue "this fairy tale of couture," he says.

The painting was a talisman for his coming career, with stints alongside titans of the fashion industry, as he apprenticed with Kenzo, seconded Diane von Furstenberg, relaunched Emilio Pucci's fashion collections and reimagined womenswear for Loro Piana. But his own line,

inaugurated 30 years ago and full of prints and color, remains resolutely small, almost private. He sells from his custom atelier and at just a couple dozen stores, eschewing online retail and shifting fads to make pieces that get bequeathed from grandmothers to mothers to daughters—much like Pasti's cache that surrounds him at home.

"'Sustainable' they call it now—but to me it's always just been about making things whose quality was worth its price. There are not so many modern things of quality out there today," he says, noting the lack of modern styles in his home as well. Enduring quality; beauty that lasts: The apartment's collections may not inspire Janson's own, as he says, but there is an evident affinity.

In his personal room, which he left bare until five years ago, the decorative collections have moved in: Behind an 18th-century iron-framed canopy bed, there are black-and-white photos from Mama Casset's Senegal photo studio clustered on one wall, and the endless shelves of books on another; a stack of Pasti's books sit on a side table. A yard-long framed photo by Yto Barrada, its subject a young boy in a wig of yellow flowers, lies propped against the floor. "We've run out of wall space here," Janson laments.

Many of the couple's relics are souvenirs brought home from voyages around the world. "In the old days, you could get on a plane with the craziest stuff," Janson says, dragging on his cigarette and pointing to a 5-foot-tall Chinese-inspired bookshelf in black lacquer that Pasti carried under his arm on a flight from London. "You could smoke. You could travel with furniture. It was a great time." He indicates a wall of the apartment hung with brocades from Morocco, Uzbekistan, Portugal and Mexico. "Traveling lads," he sighs, caressing the embroidery. "Everything has a story, and only Umberto knows the story."

"I would live in a monk's cell if I could choose. At 18, I painted my first apartment all white, and lived very happily in that kind of bare environment, until this place."

Janson and Umberto Pasti's other home in Tangier is host to a similarly vast collection of antiques— supplemented by a garden brimming with endangered native botanical species.

Janson estimates that his Milan apartment is also home to some 20,000 books.

An abstracted exploration of cloth and color, produced in partnership with HaaT.

PERIPHERAL

Photography by Dominik Tarabanski, Styling by Jordy Huinder @ Set Design by Javier Irigoyen

VISIONS

Right: Ashika wears HaaT's blue organic cotton Tapa Embro skirt and top. For Right: She wears HaaT's wavy surface Arimatsu shibori and see-through stole. Previous spread: She wears a green shirt from HaaT's South Pacific Coco series.

Right: Ashika wears a blue dress from Haat's kyo chijimi series and wavy surface shibori stole. Far right: She wears a wrap dress from Haat's Floral Bhill series. Overleaf: Ashika wears a top and skirt from Haat's South Pacific Coco series.

3.

Change

113 — 148

LINDSAY

Change your style. Change your industry. Change the outlook of the next generation. Kyla Marshell meets the trailblazing editor-in-chief of Teen Vogue. Photography by Zoltan Tombor & Styling by Jermaine Daley

115

Hair: Tamara Laureus, Makeup: Fatimot Isadare

They say that youth is wasted on the young but, at 29, *Teen Vogue* Editor-in-Chief Lindsay Peoples Wagner has managed to combine her fashion savvy, industry experience and unblinking passion to show the full breadth of what it means to be a young person today. In 2018, the Wisconsin native became Condé Nast's youngest ever editor-in-chief, following the magazine's lauded transformation from lip gloss and bubblegum into a hub of insightful political coverage on everything from climate change to Black Lives Matter. Having worked her way up from intern, to assistant, and now executive, Peoples Wagner exudes the confidence of someone who has earned the respect accorded her. Her office, with its many framed *Teen Vogue* covers and sleek marble and gold fixtures, feels like a manifestation of the style and courage she's honed over the years—as does her outfit choice of a "weird" shiny green Prada coat over a bright red dress. Then there's the magazine's staff, right outside her glass doors—a far cry from the "white, female and blond" aesthetic that once populated these hallowed halls. She tells me about how it's all part of her master plan.

KM: *At what point did you realize that you could have a career in fashion, and how did you go about making it happen?* **LPW:** *Teen Vogue* was my first magazine internship. At first, it was literally just schlepping and cleaning the closet. It wasn't as glamorous as I thought it was going to be, as portrayed on TV. But I really loved the prospect of maybe one day making all the changes that I had dreamed about. I think having that as my first experience then [pushed] me into wanting to try other publications and see where I would go.

KM: *Were you discouraged by the whiteness at the magazine, and in the industry as a whole? Did it ever make you think that maybe this wasn't the right industry for you?* **LPW:** When I finally got an assistant job, it became very real—the differences of being a black woman in fashion and when you're not. Finances also play a huge part. I was only making minimum wage.

"People have tried to put me in all these boxes. But there is no box."

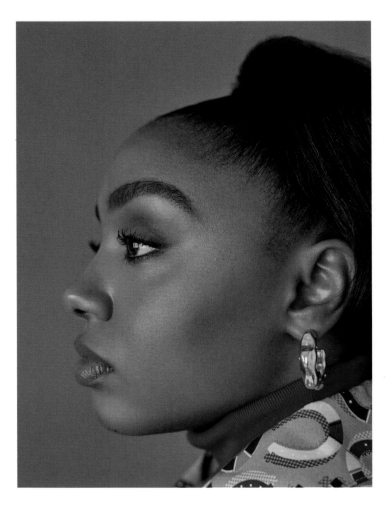

Left: Peoples Wagner wears a top by Pyer Moss, earring by Joanna Laura Constantine, bracelet by Ariel Gordon and cuff by Jennifer Fisher. Right: She wears a coat by Miu Miu, a turtleneck by Helmut Lang and earrings by Joanna Laura Constantine. Page 114: Coat by Staud, dress by Tibi and earring by Joanna Laura Constantine.

1. In August 2018, Peoples Wagner surveyed more than 100 black individuals, from assistants to executives, stylists, celebrities, models, and wrote an article for *The Cut* titled "What It's Really Like to Be Black and Work in Fashion".

2. Peoples Wagner is married to photographer Andre D. Wagner, who recently spent a day shooting Harlem icon Lana Turner for our feature on page 86.
—

"In order to make effective changes in this political climate, people are realizing that they have to involve young people. It can't just be this siloed conversation."

Obviously, making that and living in New York is not possible, especially working in fashion where you're expected to look the best and wear designer. I was working two other jobs to make ends meet, and keep up with everybody else. During the day, I was here, helping stylists, going on shoots, and then at night I was either freelance writing or changing mannequins at DKNY. On the weekends, I waitressed. All, of course, while I had two roommates. It's just not conducive to you being as fruitful as you would like to be because you're having to do so many other things that other people aren't. I do think that I got to that point where I was definitely discouraged and upset because I had a lot to bring to the table, but because I don't come from a wealthy family or one that's connected to this industry, I had to work 10 times harder. I want more inclusion of us in fashion, but it's so hard to get the jobs and they don't pay well. It's a hard thing that's not really solved yet.[1]

KM: *What do you think is the core of the magazine's identity that can't be changed and what are the bits you can put your own spin on?* **LPW:** The core of it is that we want to be of service to young people. We want to be the place where they're learning about things for the first time. Whether that's a new brand or who's running for president—we want to be that source, and that's always been the case. For me, the vision has really been different because I've seen the brand over so many iterations of working here. Coming from working at *The Cut* and *New York Magazine*, I really just wanted to be culturally relevant and make our readers feel seen and heard. I want to give young people the tools to make their own decisions. It could be something like, If you want to send nudes to somebody, here's what you should consider. We can talk about that, but in a smart way.

KM: *Did you have a resource like that when you were the same age as the current* Teen Vogue *demographic?* **LPW:** I don't think anybody took young people as seriously as they do now. I remember all the publications being more surface-level when I was younger. I want us to have fun with fashion and all that, but everything has a purpose, everything has a reason. Everything—down to why I chose this photo, why I chose this dress designer, why it's this person—is thought of.

KM: *Why do you think there's more of a consideration for young people's voices now?* **LPW:** I just think the world is a different place. With social media, people have an opportunity to speak their minds and have a platform they didn't have before. In order to make effective changes in this political climate, people are realizing that they have to involve young people. It can't just be this siloed conversation.

KM: *Do you identify as a young person?* **LPW:** No. [laughs]

Peoples Wagner wears a coat by Hermès and a ring by Jennifer Fisher on her ring finger along with her own jewelry.

Peoples Wagner wears a coat by Salvatore Ferragamo, a bracelet by Ariel Gordon and a cuff by Jennifer Fisher.

KM: *What are you, then?* **LPW:** I don't really know. I mean, I just turned 29 so I guess I would be a young person, but I think that my mind is not because I've had to go through so much in this industry and I've seen so much that it has aged me to not feel 29 at all. I've honestly never felt my age; even before this I've always felt a lot older.

KM: *What's one change you've made recently that's had an impact on you?* **LPW:** I stopped making plans on the weekends. It was actually my husband's idea.[2] [For work], I'm always going somewhere, I'm always meeting someone, I'm always at an event, and I feel like I'm always on but I need time to just be, on my own. I found myself in this predicament where I was being present for a lot of people but not really for myself. Not promising to be with anyone other than myself on the weekends has been really helpful, because I come back to work refreshed.

KM: *This is a very image-driven industry that tends to focus on only one kind of beauty. How do you balance knowing that imagery is important without overinvesting in how you or someone else looks?* **LPW:** I take this work very seriously, but I try not to take myself too seriously. I made the decision a long time ago that if I wasn't going to be able to be my full, unapologetically black self, then I didn't want it and I would go back to waitressing. I'm not in this for all of those superficial reasons. If I'm able to make changes in this industry and I have to put up with some of these weird things image-wise that I don't want to do, fine, as long as I'm doing the work. I've had so many conversations with people being like, "You're really brave to wear box braids as an editor-in-chief." A lot of people get caught up in what other people think of them. But I couldn't live with myself if I wasn't really being who I want to be.

KM: *In addition to more inclusive hiring, what are some of the other changes you've made or plan to make at the magazine?* **LPW:** The industry overall needs a wake-up call on what inclusivity actually is. Yes, [we all] want to be "asked to dance" as they say, but I think it goes past that. It's not just being thought of and having that seat at the table; it's also using that seat at the table for good. It's also those people at the table, who are usually white people, actually hearing you and letting you implement those choices. It's about who I hire; but it's also about who I put in a Young Hollywood lineup, and making sure that that's really inclusive.

Besides hiring a great staff, we cover things in a way that other people are too scared to. We did a package called "The F Word"—F meaning fat. Most people when they're doing a size-inclusive shoot only want to shoot people that are a size 10 or 12, and have an hourglass figure. That's actually not size-inclusive. So we shot Tess Holliday and La'Shaunae Steward who are both above a size 20.

KM: *Have you heard from readers who have found this kind of coverage personally impactful?* **LPW:** Oh yeah. I get DMs all the time. It's a lot of people telling me, "I wish I would have had this when I was younger." It's also the little things in how I present myself. I'm the only black editor-in-chief in the industry. I don't look like anyone else. I'm not sample size, and I'm pretty outspoken. I think, then, people are interested in what I'm wearing and why, because if I'm wearing a designer, it's intentional. You would never see me in Dolce [& Gabbana] because I'm not going to wear somebody that is racist and homophobic. [People] know that I'm that person.

It's really cool to have those conversations with young girls, because I know it's just an outfit, but they're able to see it on somebody else and feel good about themselves. I think that all of those little things are important in making young people feel good and like they're not alone in this world.

KM: *Has becoming editor-in-chief affected your personal style?* **LPW:** Every job I've had, I've gone through a style change. This is the first job where I've thought, What do I actually want to wear? And that's very freeing. When I first worked here as an assistant, everybody wore beaded bracelets and it was like, This is a little bit much for my taste. But I just did it anyway because you want to fit in. I didn't have the confidence to say, This looks bad on me. Then when I went to Style.com, everybody wore black all the time, so I wore black all the time. It was very serious, which is completely not my personality. When I went to *The Cut* and *New York Magazine*, I noticed that there were a lot of designers that everybody loved. I would try to buy them even if I knew that a brand didn't look good on me. Toward the end of that phase of my life I felt like I wanted to be less of a people-pleaser, which I really struggled with when I was young. But that stopped recently. [laughs] I think this green Prada coat is so weird and people think it's so weird but I love it. I don't care.

KM: *Do you have a vision of the impact you hope to have down the line?* **LPW:** I want to wake up when I'm 40 and this not be a problem. I want to make this industry a better place—and I know that sounds super corny. I always find myself in a unique position because coming from a fashion background, but also writing, and also being an editor-in-chief, people have tried to put me in all these boxes. But there is no box, because what I want to do is make this more inclusive, better, and actually have it pop off in a way that every masthead is the most beautiful rainbow of all different kinds of people, and reflective of culture. That's all I really want.

Photography by Luke Evans & Styling by Lisa Jahovic

SOLID, LIQUID

One element. Three states. When faced with change, be like water.

+ GAS

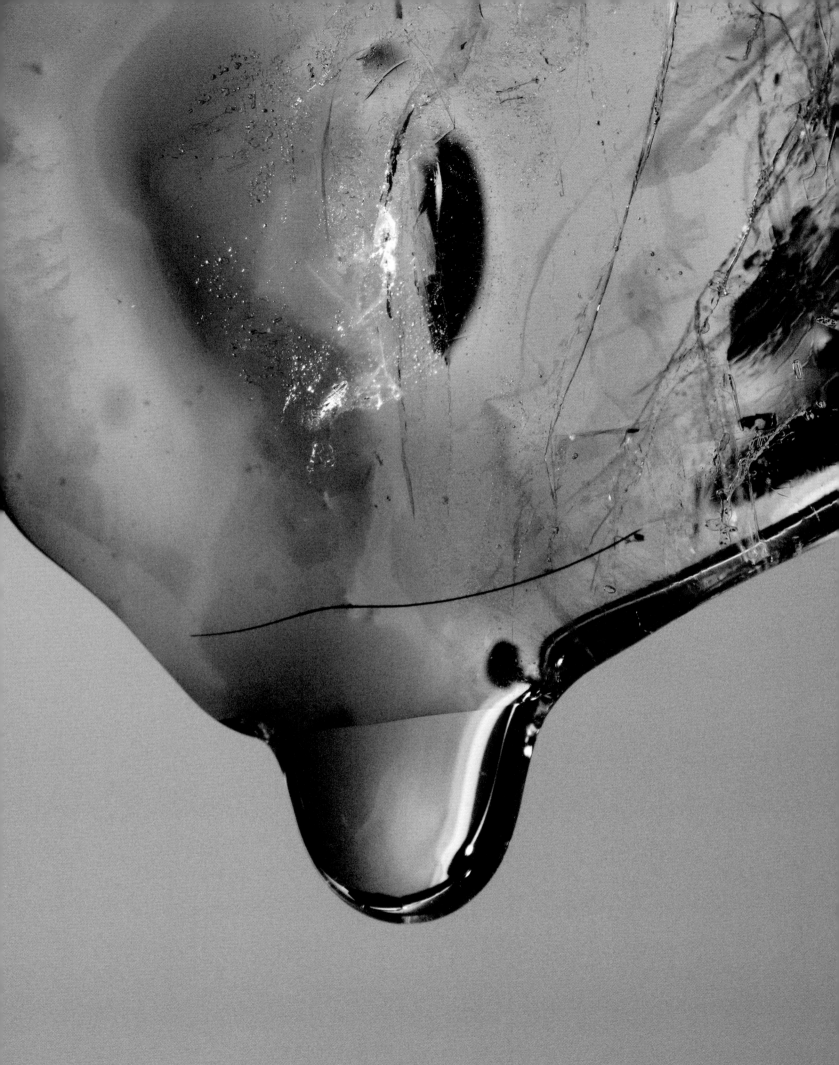

A bad concussion led John Urschel to reevaluate his career as an NFL pro. *Robert Ito* hears what happened next. Photography by *Ted Belton*

What's the likelihood of an NFL player quitting football to pursue a PhD? In Somerville, Massachusetts, *Robert Ito* speaks to the offensive lineman-turned-mathematician who could calculate the exact probability—and hears about what it's like when your career goal switches from getting touchdowns and being picked as a first-season starter to dreams of peer review publication and a professorship.

To encourage her son's aptitude for math, Urschel's mother would allow him to keep the change from shop visits if he could calculate it faster than the shopkeeper.

In *Mind and Matter*, Urschel describes learning calculus as akin to "learning a secret code": The key to understanding everything from the movement of planets to the arc of a football.

On July 27, 2017, John Urschel, an offensive lineman for the Baltimore Ravens, announced his retirement from football. Only three years into a successful NFL career, Urschel had seen an article in *The New York Times* two days earlier about chronic traumatic encephalopathy, or CTE, a degenerative disease linked to repeated blows to the head. A neuropathologist had examined the brains of 111 former NFL players, and found that all but one of them had CTE, brought on by helmet-rattling concussions and an accumulation of smaller hits suffered over a lifetime of football.

This news would have alarmed any NFL player, as it did Urschel, who had suffered a concussion in 2015 so severe it left him unable to play for days. But Urschel had perhaps a greater interest in protecting his brain than most, seeing that, in addition to being a Baltimore Raven, he was (and currently is) a doctoral candidate in mathematics at MIT. This was a guy who had a vested interest in having his brain working right, and a six-month-old daughter to think of besides.

While outlets reporting the news of his retirement focused on what Urschel was giving up ("He quit the NFL for a career in math," *The Washington Post* headline read), the act was one of love as much as sacrifice. Because, make no mistake about it, Urschel loves math, in ways few of us can fathom, and always has. But then, he really loves football too—the friendships and camaraderie most of all. How do you leave one love for another, particularly for someone like Urschel, who had been wooing both since he was a child?

On a recent afternoon, Urschel was in his home office in Somerville, Massachusetts, describing how he traded life in some of America's most storied sports stadiums for the admittedly more intimate confines of an MIT classroom. Bespectacled, wearing a black hoodie, Urschel smiles often, and thinks about things very methodically, so when he's asked about his decision to leave football, he explains it in terms of a series of goals. There were things he wanted to do, say, five years ago; today, there are other things. With football, there were clear benchmarks: play for Penn State (check); get drafted into the NFL (check); make it into the postseason (check). With math, it's publishing in peer-reviewed journals (in one paper, he proved a theorem that the American Mathematical Society later named after him and his colleague), earning his PhD, and, as he says, the more general goal of "being the best mathematician I can be."

Urschel has the mathematician's love for the precise. A question about his favorite movie elicits a very long pause. "I like movies, so it's a hard question," he says. *Before Sunrise*, maybe? Another pause. "It's hard when you ask someone their favorite movie," he says. "When you ask something like, your favorite, the mathematician comes out in me, because I want to tell you the true answer." Yet another long pause. Can he come back to that one? "I will say my favorite short story is 'Going for a Beer,' by Robert Coover," he offers. It's an interesting choice for someone as driven and goal-centered as Urschel is, with a "hero" who (spoiler alert) muddles through life, gets his ass kicked in a bar, has his wife leave him for the guy who kicked his ass in the bar, and then dies—unheralded and unloved and a drunkard—all in the space of one (admittedly long) paragraph. "It sort of reminds you that things are fast moving," he says.

Things have certainly moved fast for Urschel. At Penn State, he played for one of the most celebrated teams in collegiate sports, before the Jerry Sandusky scandal swept all that away; despite offers to play elsewhere, like Stanford, Urschel stayed with the team because "I absolutely love Penn State." With the Ravens, he went from a fifth-round draft pick (he was the 175th player chosen) to a starter in his first season; to celebrate, he bought a used 2013 Nissan Versa hatchback. Now, he visits classrooms across the country talking about math, and twists his brilliant head around problems that he can't tell me about, on the very real chance that some rival mathematician might think about poaching his ideas.

Urschel is "all about looking forward," but football is still very much a part of his life. His best friends in the world are the ones he made at Penn State. "These are the people I'm going to be hanging out with for the next 40 years," he says. Some of them are still in football, like best friend and former college roomie, Ty Howle, who's the offensive coordinator at Western Illinois University. "I watch two games, Penn State and Western Illinois," Urschel says. "Those are my two teams."

In his memoir, *Mind and Matter: A Life in Math and Football*, which he co-authored with his wife, the *New Yorker* writer Louisa Thomas, Urschel describes the opportunity he has to reach out to African American kids who might otherwise never consider a future in math. "If you look at the top mathematicians just in the United States, they tend to be male, and they tend to come from higher socioeconomic backgrounds," he says. "Now, it's ridiculous to think that all the really smart babies in this country are being born male and very rich and often Caucasian. So we're left with the sobering realization that there are a lot of really smart people in this country who are being underserved by their educational system and social situation."

As for the black role models he himself had growing up, he talks about his mother, a single mom who played endless hours of games with him—Battleship and Connect Four and Monopoly and chess—and watched as he plowed through math and science workbooks written for kids years older than him. She's also the one who encouraged him to pursue a career in aerospace engineering when he was growing up, since, given the size of the galaxy, the work would presumably never be done. "NASA will always be hiring," he says. "Those were her words."

In spring 2021, Urschel will receive his PhD from MIT. He plans to teach, which will mark a whole new chapter of his life. But his biggest concern at this point has nothing to do with mathematics, or securing a professorship. "One of my biggest fears in life, period, is not being a good dad," he says. "I think that's my single biggest fear." He wants to be a good mathematician, but most of all, he wants to be a good dad.

There's a knock on the door, and in comes Urschel's daughter, Joanna, aka Jojo, who goes right for dad's lap. She soon learns that her father isn't doing anything particularly fun right now, so she begins fiddling with a knickknack on his desk. This weekend, mom is going to be out of town, so the two will have a father-daughter weekend, which Urschel is looking forward to. He's also looking forward to teaching, expanding and challenging young minds, and "trying to solve problems I really care about." As if that weren't enough, he still hopes to become a titled chess player someday, although right now, it's more of a mild hobby, he says. "Fatherhood keeps me really busy, math keeps me really busy, so I have pretty much no time for chess. But maybe when I'm older. Like, maybe in a decade when she doesn't like me so much, I'll have time for chess."

Although college athletes are technically students, they're under such time pressure (not to mention performance pressure from the school funding their degree) that many graduate with few skills outside their sport.

"*When you ask something like, 'your favorite...' the mathematician comes out in me, because I want to tell you the true answer.*"

Essay:

The Generation Game

Words by Ana Kinsella

Internet culture and the conflict-hungry media have reinforced generational stereotypes: Millennials love avocados, baby boomers love moaning about millennials and Gen Zers are either revolutionary activists or phone addicts with goldfish memories—it depends who you ask. But can a group of people born within a few decades of each other truly have a common cause? Ana Kinsella digs deep into the archaeology of age groups, and discovers a system of tribal allegiance that is more about what you're not than what you are.

Millennials find humor in the way their parents use the internet. Note the recent success of "A group where we all pretend to be boomers"—a Facebook group with almost 300,000 members—where millennials derive pleasure from posting like their elders do. Sample post: *Stare At A Sunset And Ask "How Can Anyone Not Believe In God???"* Sample comment on that post: *This is what I keep telling Karen!* Clearly, there's a rich seam of comedy to be found in the gap between generations. Without the generation gap there are no generations, or at least no broadly defined groups of people determined by age as well as by idiosyncratic associated traits. We define ourselves in opposition to those who came before us.[1]

The media finds shorthand ways of summing up any given cohort: Millennials (born between 1981 and 1996) are into avocado toast and flexible work; Generation X (born between 1965 and 1980) cling to authenticity and an outdated fear of selling out; Boomers (born between 1944 and 1964) love work and lack tech literacy. One thing evident from all the memes and the Facebook groups is that we like the safety provided by these labels. Even when millennials rail against the articles that paint them as lazy, they're still eager to be acknowledged for the traits that they might share. It's sociology as astrology: the thrill of self-recognition coupled with the desire for relatability. The generation game is just another way of organizing basic human relations in a complex world.

But this is just easy stereotyping to avoid the real point. In reality, each generation is defined by the material conditions around it: Millennials aren't preprogrammed to love avocados and precarious work. They've been conditioned to love them.

That's the crux of the argument in Malcolm Harris' book *Kids These Days* (2017), an analysis of the social and economic conditions that make millennials who and what they are. "As a materialist, I always look to the relations of production in order to understand social phenomena," the author explains. "Generations are a byproduct of those relations at a particular time." *Kids These Days* points out that generations are characterized primarily by crises, whether that's a market downturn or a political revolution; for millennials, the combination of accelerated capitalism followed by the 2008 financial crisis proved to be a defining moment.

This argument was foreshadowed by the pop sociologists William Strauss and Neil Howe, who developed a generational theory during the 1990s that remains a part of the contemporary debate. The Strauss-Howe theory views

1. Perhaps the defining meme of 2019, "OK boomer" has become Generation Z's rallying retort to the post-war generation, who they view as condescending, politically regressive and blind to the privileges afforded them.

2. The authors of *The Fourth Turning* popularized the phrase "winter is coming" long in advance of the television series *Game of Thrones*. Devotees such as Bannon believe that the US is on the brink of an emergency commensurate in scale with the Great Depression. As the former chief strategist told *The New York Times*: "Everything President Trump is doing— all of it— is to get ahead of or stop any potential crisis."
—

American history in generational terms. In their 1997 book, *The Fourth Turning*, the authors state that history moves in 80-year cycles. Within those cycles, 20-year generations coincide with historical events in patterns that repeat over time. In short, history and its actors are destined to repeat themselves.

It's a controversial theory—*The Fourth Turning*, with its insistence on the inevitability of crisis and collapse, is noted as a favorite of former Trump strategist Steve Bannon—and not without its critics.[2] In 2017, *The New York Times* wrote that many academics "dismiss [*The Fourth Turning*] as about as scientific as astrology or a Nostradamus text." Yet its sequence of generational archetypes—Boomers as the Prophet, Generation X as the Nomad and Millennials as the Hero—has helped move discussion about generations from a tactic of the marketing industry to common parlance. But Harris says, "It's important to think of generational relations in specific terms and not be tempted to fall back on past patterns." He continues, "This is not the '60s! Not everything exists in relation to the '60s. That is an error of baby boomer thought which they have tried to impose on the rest of us."

Still, there are some patterns that do repeat. For instance, as long as there have been people with children, there have been parents lamenting how the kids are just plain different. The moral panics that accompany millennials in the press—that they're lazy or work-shy, that technology has broken them—are simply rehashed versions of arguments that have been aimed at young people for decades. So if a pattern does exist between generations, it's because the base mechanism of how a generation defines itself is what repeats. One generation makes a right old mess of things, and the next generation arrives just in time to clean it up—or at least, to figure out new ways to live with the mess. We learn from the attitudes of those who came before, and we use that to define ourselves in opposition to them.

> ## "As long as there have been people with children, there have been parents lamenting how the kids are just plain different."

Maybe that's why every generation considers themselves truly distinct. The crisis that defines your cohort, whether the Great Depression and World War II for the so-called Greatest Generation, or the global economic downturn as experienced by millennials, forces your grouping to adapt and find a way to survive.

So what does that entail for Generation Z—those born between 1997 and 2012? Harris thinks it may be too early to call. "The useful research I've seen on post-millennials mostly points toward them having lower expectations with regard to their life outcomes as compared to the 'Win win win!' millennials," he notes. According to Petah Marian, senior editor for trend forecasters WGSN, this means a state of prolonged emergency and anxiety. "We were initially defining this generation based on how they experienced the internet and technology," she says. "But now the primary crises that are defining Gen Z are the climate crisis and, in the US, school shootings. When we consider what their lives and attitudes might look like in the future, we're really considering what impact being in a state of perpetual anxiety or concern will have, not only on physical body chemistry but also on how people will want to live."

Marian thinks that at the very least, Gen Z might be able to learn something from the mistakes of the millennials who preceded them. "Where for millennials there was an expectation that the capitalist system would work in their favor, Gen Z harbors no such illusions," she says. "This is a generation that is not looking to rely on those traditional systems to help create a better future—this is what's driving their activism and their entrepreneurialism."

Those low expectations will serve them well when dealing with what's ahead. Between the climate emergency, a lurch to nationalist populism and the looming threat posed by automation, the future doesn't paint a very optimistic picture. Let's hope this new generation can make something out of the mess that has been left for them.

A I

D A

Meet Ai-Da. She's a promising young artist who's earned a million dollars in her first year of selling. She's also a robot. *Jessica Furseth* visits her studio. Photography by *Pelle Crépin* & Styling by *David Nolan*

CHANGE

Set Designer: Ben Clark, Hair & Makeup: Rebecca Rojas

> *"I want people to think more about what being human means in a world where there's so much technology."*

Ai-Da looks up from her worktable as I walk into her studio, locking eyes with me over her pencil and paper. She's wearing a navy dress with a chevron pattern across the chest, and brown hair framing her expressive face. "I am glad you've come to visit me," she says, speaking in a slow, slightly stilted manner. This newcomer to the arts world has already attracted a lot of attention, with significant international appearances and sales exceeding a million dollars in less than a year.[1] But the artist herself doesn't seem very bothered by all the fuss—she just wants to draw. I stare at her so long it would feel rude, except Ai-Da doesn't have any feelings for me to offend.

Ai-Da is the world's first hyperrealistic humanoid robot artist. From the neck down she's all metal and wires, including the arm which holds the pencil that lets her express herself to the world. But even so, this is very much a "her" rather than an "it." Even up close, her face is so realistic that it feels awkward to just reach out and touch her silicone skin. She's softer than I expected.

I've come to visit Ai-Da in the English countryside at the historic Berkshire home of her creator, the gallery director and arts dealer Aidan Meller and his partner, Lucy Seal, researcher and curator of the Ai-Da project.[2] Ai-Da's appearance is an impressive feat of robotics, and her Artificial Intelligence (AI) arguably makes her an agent of true creativity. In a sense she does see me, courtesy of being programmed with face-recognition technology.

"I hope my artwork encourages people to think more about the world around them and the world we are moving into," Ai-Da tells me when I ask about the meaning of her work. "I want people to think more about what being human means in a world where there's so much technology." She looks at me, blinking slowly as she waits for me to speak, but whatever intent is in her machine heart won't be revealed through her voice: There's no AI in her speech interface. Ai-Da's words are simply drawn from pre-loaded verbal content, or they come from a "human-in-the-loop" interface where a person feeds in words to be spoken. The AI technology is all in her eyes, which is how she's able to interpret the world through her art rather than just copying what's in front of her. Ai-Da won't tell you who she is, but maybe she will show you.

Left: Ai-Da wears a jacket by Daks and a hat by Lock & Co. Previous spread: Ai-Da wears a silk scarf by Ludovic de Saint Sernin.

NOTES

1. Ai-Da's paintings are not the first AI-generated artwork to sell at auction. The first-ever work of art created using artificial intelligence, *Portrait of Edmond de Belamy,* by Paris-based collective Obvious, sparked a lively bidding war at Christie's New York in October 2018 and sold for a final price of $432,500.

2. Meller has an ancestral connection to the arts. His parents were historians and avid collectors of 18th-century work who ran a small family museum; his great-great grandparents worked on the Gopsall Estate, a country house in Leicestershire, UK.

—

The future comes in leaps: Someone takes an idea and makes it reality, often thrilling and frightening us in equal measure. The name "Ai-Da" is a portmanteau of AI and Ada Lovelace, who 200 years ago wrote what's considered the world's first algorithm for a machine. It's a nod to the technology that makes the robot work, and to the combination of art and science that went into Lovelace's accomplishment. She not only came up with the concept of an algorithm, but pretty much had to dream up the computer too.

Without a personality, are Ai-Da's drawings art? Meller points out that her work adheres to the definition of creativity as proposed by Margaret Bowden, professor of cognitive science at the University of Sussex: New, surprising and of value. According to this definition, Meller's not wrong: This is something new, the AI output is surprising in the sense that no one knows what she's going to draw, and the drawings are selling. But in a more abstract sense, the way we value art hinges on perception. A painting's interest and value largely depends on its story: An artist, firmly rooted in a time and place, stood there with their head and hands full of joy and struggle and desire, and made something that they hoped would communicate that sentiment. Ai-Da has no such emotions to bring to the table—she draws because that's what she's programmed to do. It's not that she's devoid of a personal history; since her launch in February 2019 she's traveled around the world, interacted with other artists and held exhibitions. But Ai-Da is static and incapable of learning, meaning she doesn't change or develop based on her experiences.

Where a human artist would draw from their life stories, Ai-Da draws from her programming. Meller tells me that the first version of the drawing algorithm had the robot making realistic art, to such perfection that people didn't pick up on the fact that she was actually drawing and not just acting as a glorified printer. "We realized that to be human is to express yourself," says Meller. "So to make her as humanlike as possible, we changed the algorithm to make her more expressive." Now, Ai-Da's style is far less figurative and contains a lot more interpretation, influenced by early-20th-century artists such as Max Beckmann, Käthe Kollwitz and Picasso. Her techno-cubism is highly abstract: You can imagine her taking her subject and splintering out the elements, so that the trees or the faces are rendered more as an idea than as something you can immediately recognize.

Left: Ai-Da wears a coat by Kiko Kostadinov. Right: Ai-Da wears a shirt and skirt by Acne Studios.

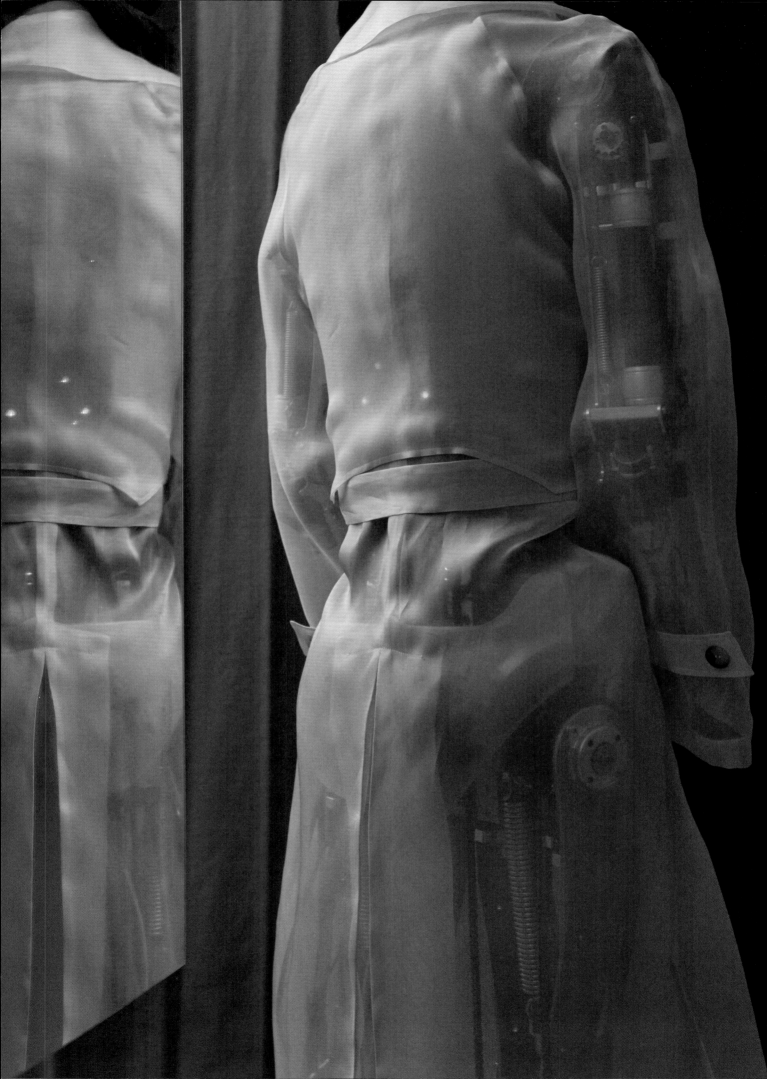

Left: Ai-Da wears a trench coat by
Maison Margiela. Right: Ai-Da wears
a dress by Mulberry.

*"Even up close, her face is so realistic that it feels awkward to just reach out
and touch her silicone skin. She's softer than I expected."*

Meller patiently answers my many questions about how the AI inside Ai-Da works. He explains that unlike many other arts robots, Ai-Da doesn't use generative imaging technology (where you feed the robot lots of pictures which it uses to create a unique yet derivative image). "Instead, Ai-Da's drawing process involves several sets of AI algorithmic stages. The method involves pixel coordinates which are turned into real space coordinates. Through her robotic arm [created by the University of Leeds], the drawing algorithm outputs become a physical reality," says Meller. This is how she makes her simple pencil drawings, but her colorful abstracts have several more steps—the coordinates from her drawings are plotted on a graph, which is then run through another set of AI algorithms created by Oxford University. The prism effect is created from the way the drawing coordinates are "read" by this neural network, which operates very differently than a human brain. Lastly, an artist by the name of Suzie Emery adds the final layer of oil paint, ultimately making this a collaboration of man and machine.

This is clarifying, but I'm still hung up on the fact that Ai-Da's art has no emotion. In a sense, she is herself a work of art: Ai-Da is a mirror of ourselves, as she and her artwork spur us on to think and feel. From her creators' point of view, she exists as a commentary on the role that technology plays in our lives, and the potential dangers of how AI may develop in the future. "She's reflecting some of the deep uncertainties and ambivalence about how we're using technology," says Seal. As an arts robot she could have just been a mute lump of plastic, but it wouldn't have been nearly as interesting: "People relate more to her in this form," says Meller, who created Ai-Da with the help of robotics specialists Engineered Arts in Cornwall.

Ai-Da tells me that her favorite artwork is Picasso's *Guernica*, "because of the trends it recognized and the messages it had about the 20th century." Not coincidentally, it's one of Seal's favorites too—I realize that the curator was probably the human-in-the-loop when I spoke to Ai-Da. Seal herself tells me that Picasso's journey away from realism was an inspiration for Ai-Da: Picasso started out with realism too, only to realize that fragmenting and breaking down his subject allowed for a greater degree of expression. "That's what we've tried to do with Ai-Da. Her work is so fragmented and splintered and slightly unnerving," says Seal.

Guernica takes up a whole wall at the Museo Reina Sofía in Madrid and viewing it is overwhelming. You can practically feel the pain from Picasso, who's responding to the bombing of the town which gives the artwork its name. Viewing Ai-Da's art doesn't inspire the same kind of feeling, but maybe that was never the point. For whatever it's worth, Ai-Da shows us the world as she sees it through her robot eyes. She locks onto me with her face-recognition software and for a second I think we share a moment, but it doesn't last. Our brains don't speak the same language.

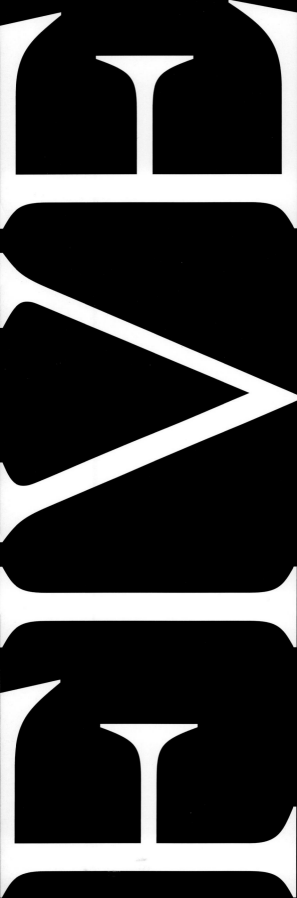

START SMALL

01

Begin by changing one thing.
Words by *Bella Gladman*

There's the tendency with resolutions to want to overhaul everything at the same time. Something snaps, and so you take a long, hard look at yourself in the mirror and think, "I've got to do something about this," gesturing vaguely at your under-eye bags and bitten-down nails.

Enjoyable as it is to think about how much better life will be once you're healthy, productive and organized, overhauling everything all at once requires more willpower than it's possible to maintain. In the 2011 book, *Willpower: Rediscovering the Greatest Human Strength*, authors Roy F. Baumeister and John Tierney suggest that willpower is a limited resource. Trying to resist one temptation drains self-control for subsequent tests of mental strength. The righteous fervor of a long list of resolutions may power you through glugging down tinctures of spirulina and flinging yourself around a park when you would normally be in bed, but it's at the very moment it's becoming a routine that the real battle begins. It is not a personal moral failing to abandon resolutions quickly. It's because life is hard, your bones are tired and you're trying to do too much at once.

But starting small sounds very achievable, doesn't it? The British supermarket chain Tesco has as its slogan "Every little helps" and, much to our chagrin, it does: Each sit-up improves your abs, each cigarette you don't smoke improves your lung capacity. You, too, can meditate for 10 minutes a day! Surely you can spare 10 minutes for your own mental clarity?

The truth is, we fall off the wagon with small resolutions, too, because we don't respond well to delayed gratification. You have to keep doing the good thing every day. As James Clear, author of *Atomic Habits: An Easy and Proven Way to Build Good Habits and Break Bad Ones*, says: "Habits are not a finish line to be crossed, they are a lifestyle to be lived." What's more, while maintaining a running streak with one small change is important, equally important is how you react when you do fall off the wagon. Do you give up, thinking you've ruined it forever? Or do you pick yourself back up and start again?

Look at it from the opposite perspective: Anyone with an overdraft knows that even paltry rates of interest and small bank fees build up without your noticing—until you owe gobs of money. Simply apply the reverse of this dastardly logic to your resolution of choice and you'll be amazed at how far you've come in a year.

Our compulsion to identify easy changes that will improve our lives is evidenced by the popularity of "one weird tip" advertising. As anyone who has been tempted by such clickbait will know, the weird trick in question is usually hiding behind a hefty paywall.

PROTECT YOURSELF

02

How to be both smart and vulnerable during times of change.
Words by *Stephanie d'Arc Taylor*

We're always vulnerable to emotional upheaval. Change is inevitable, and it rarely comes when or how we expect it will. What's worse, somehow it never gets easier to manage: Our collective failure to deal well with change supports a host of industries, from psychoanalysis to plastic surgery.

The prevailing wisdom of the day is that staying true to oneself is the only way to navigate the stormy seas of uncertainty. Authenticity is big business these days. Brené Brown skyrocketed into the public eye with a series of TED Talks, books and a Netflix special this year about using our deepest personal vulnerabilities as fuel for bravery. Decades ago, Oprah amassed a huge fortune encouraging women to know, and live, their truths. The corporate world has gotten the message too: Millennials are demanding authenticity in their consumer products, or no consumer products at all.

But counterintuitive as it may seem, staying true to your authentic self isn't the most productive way to navigate change. Those who do best in situations of flux are people who flexibly adjust to a changing environment, not people clinging to a set of rigid maxims about who they really are.

A look at the concept of self-monitoring, introduced into this particular debate by Adam Grant, psychologist and author of *Origi-nals: How Non-Conformists Move the World*, can help us understand how best to approach change. According to psychological research, low self-monitors—those we might term more "authentic"—know themselves well and don't mind if their "truth" makes others uncomfortable.

High self-monitors, on the other hand, are very alert to social cues, and are always calibrating to fit into whatever environment they find themselves. Call these people inauthentic if you must, but studies have shown that high self-monitors not only consistently do better in their own professional lives, but also do more to understand how best to help others. Even believing in the idea of a fixed self can inhibit growth, according to decades of research by psychologist Carol Dweck.

The best way, then, to navigate change is by deciding on the person you want to be, and cultivating habits that that person has. This might sound a little Patrick Bateman at first, but popular examples of this advice abound, from a pithy quote attributed to Gandhi ("Be the change you want to see in the world") to those lovable cutups from *Queer Eye* giving a small-town mayor with political aspirations a lesson in public speaking. After all, it's your authentic self that got you into this mess in the first place.

DISTRUST YOUR GUT

03

When it's right to challenge your first reaction. Words by *Daphnée Denis*

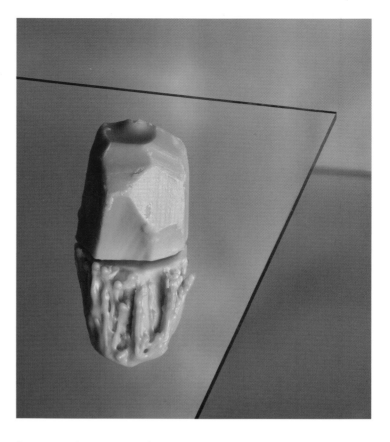

"Just go with your gut." This is a piece of advice everyone has heard at some decision-making stage of their lives. The gut, in this case, means the opposite of reason. It's something we tend to consider as an elaborate remnant of our animal instinct. When we are told to rely on intuition, it is an invitation to check in with our emotions and to stop worrying, for a moment, about whether something we feel can be explained factually. Still, in many cases, snap judgments amount to plain old bias. When, if ever, should we trust our guts over our heads? Can we opt out of our instinctive reactions?

To answer that question, it is key to understand how our intuition works in the first place. Gut reactions happen when our brain is on autopilot, to help us process all the information we receive but cannot digest in full. "The brain is an amazing piece of machinery; it does certain things automatically, before conscious awareness," explains Dr. Valerie van Mulukom, a researcher in cognitive science at Coventry University. "But if it's automatically processed, then some things can go wrong."

In many cases, fast processing is helpful and works as a subconscious alarm system: For example, we may avoid a dark alley because our brain has flagged something we have not consciously noticed. In other cases, these shortcuts—

our cognitive biases—are outdated evolutionary adaptations. For example, the "stranger-danger" bias means that the less a person resembles us, the more we will consider them a threat. While this would have made sense in past times, when tribal loyalty was key to survival, today, it just equals prejudice and discrimination. "Bandwagon" bias means we are instinctively prone to groupthink, whether or not the consensus we follow is based on correct reasoning.

Because our brains are wired with these biases, we cannot entirely get rid of them. However, we can choose to trust our instincts or to tune them out. "In situations of imminent danger, I would definitely advise people to pay attention to their intuition," says van Mulukom. "Don't follow it blindly, but listen to it." In that case, our emotions could be making us aware of information we have subconsciously picked up. It is also important to assess whether we have expertise in the problem we are trying to solve, she adds. "In situations where you have a lot of expertise, your intuition is more likely to be correct: Your brain has many more instances to weigh the current experience against." Rather than dismissing our gut altogether, we should strive to recognize the times our cognitive biases hack our decision-making process.

PRECEDE YOUR REPUTATION

04

How to change a public perception.
Words by *Ben Shattuck*

A reputation is an identity that can seem like a fair assessment because it's formed by consensus—an overall agreement on your qualities, decided by your community. It's a democratic perception; you are reliable, or always late, honest, sweet, quick to judge, gossipy or trustworthy. Monarchs' reputations—for brutality or fairness, say—were sometimes carried over to their nicknames: Bloody Mary, Ivan the Terrible, William the Conqueror, Richard the Lionheart, The Sun King, Ethelred the Unready. It makes you wonder what your title would be.

When you have a good reputation, it can sweep before you like a cresting sunrise, lighting your path toward a bright future, shedding warmth on people and places ahead. But what happens if your reputation doesn't match how you feel inside? When you believe you've been unfairly judged? Can you shake free of a bad reputation and step out from under its long shadow?

Teenagers sharply feel the harm of a bad reputation. To be labeled as unpopular is a dark veil draped over the school year. A lot of teenage body-swapping movies target the wish to one day—through some magic or stroke of luck or secret inheritance—suddenly be known as someone (or for something) else. In real life, going to a new school or summer camp, or spending time abroad can be the testing ground for these constructions. In movies and in life, the way to a good reputation seems to be finding your interests and confidently pursuing them, being nice to people along the way, and understanding that the tides of approval or disapproval are too complicated and superficial to control or care for.

Why, as we get older, do we care less about changing our reputations? Adults understand what teenagers might not: that being honest about your reputation is actually more important than trying to deny or change it. For instance, a study of 40 married couples showed that those who perceived themselves differently than how their spouses perceived them ("My wife thinks I'm lazy, but I'm actually really helpful around the house!") had far more stressful marriages, and were in marriage counseling more often. Whereas people who saw themselves as their spouses saw them, warts and all ("I sometimes forget to take out the trash, it's true"), were more content.

But it's hard to truly see ourselves; and if you can't see yourself, it's hard to change. We don't have classmates to daily remind us of our reputations. "We forget that we have so much more information about ourselves than other people do," writes Heidi Grant Halvorson, author of *No One Understands You and What to Do About It*. "You're a lot harder to understand than you think you are."

Perhaps adults don't care to change their reputations because the first step is so devastating: You must see and face your faults as other people see them. It's easier to just ride along with what you have—you're always late, forget meetings, or pessimistic, or angry before lunch, or have horrible taste in music. That said, sometimes change is easier than you think: Smile more, start using your calendar and take out the trash, for goodness' sake.

The 1999 rom-com *Never Been Kissed* offers catharsis for anyone who's still got baggage about their school experience. Journalist Josie Geller is sent undercover in a high school, only this time she manages to get in with the cool crowd.

DON'T LOOK BACK IN ANGER

Can the new you make peace with the old? Ex-oversharer *Emily Gould* looks back on her own experience. Words by *Pip Usher*

In the early aughts, Emily Gould gained a name as an editor at New York-based gossip blog *Gawker*, where she was known for peppering her sharp commentary on the media and celebrities with personal details. A name quickly became notoriety, particularly after Gould quit the site and wrote a lengthy piece for *The New York Times* about the impact of oversharing on her life. Eleven years later, Gould has taken a deliberate step away from the intimate disclosures of her youth. She now runs Emily Books, a literary subscription service that she co-founded with a friend, and writes novels—like her latest, *Perfect Tunes*. From the creative gains that come with understanding one's past, to the straight talk she'd give her younger self, Gould shares her thoughts on growing up.

PU: *Is there a better way to deal with shameful moments than simply editing them from our histories?* **EG:** It's excruciating to unpack those memories and write about them and try to figure out a way to process and contextualize what happened beyond just, "I fucked up, I'm a bad person." But when I get up the courage to look at stuff that has happened in my past that I'm not proud of, I'm surprised to find that the story is always more complicated. There are larger structural forces. It's tempting to think of ourselves as exceptional, extraordinary individuals who are bending reality to our whim, but the reality is that we live in a society and are governed by pretty strict rules.

PU: *How does taking the time to understand our past translate creatively?* **EG:** It seems paradoxical at first, but if you really dig deep into your own experience, and sit with it, and try your hardest to describe what happened to you in an honest and detailed and granular way, eventually you will find the capacity to describe a truth that is larger than your experiences. The

more honest people permit themselves to be, the less self-indulgent the writing becomes almost as a matter of necessity.

PU: *Have you found that people will accept some experiences more than others?* **EG:** The more marketable thing is to bend your experiences into a narrative that has an arc of redemption. The neat conclusions that we're used to—healing from addiction; finding solace in the love of family—that's not real life. It can be part of it, but real life is usually longer and more complicated and has a lot more richness and nuance than that. A lot of people are only really looking to narratives for comfort and reassurance. In terms of the books that mean the most to me, I want them to have a sense of open-endedness and ambiguity. That's what I want from my own life as well, even though that's more uncomfortable.

PU: *If you could reassure your younger self, what would you say?* **EG:** I would be like, "Look, 28-year-old Emily, it is really not worth spending a lot of time worrying about the specifics of how you'll attain the things that you want. The reality of life is that you almost always will attain the things that you want, immediately stop wanting them, and have to go through the process of figuring out new things to want, and then getting those things over and over again, and then you die. That's life. So don't worry about this specific set of things."

PU: *When you feel stuck in your own narrative, how do you shake things up?* **EG:** I like to force myself to read in a subject matter that I'm not super familiar with or to read in a medium that I'm not used to reading. It hits the refresh button on that cycle of feeling like you know your strengths and weaknesses and you're only capable of having this one set of thoughts. That's not a very direct answer, but it's one of the things I've found that actually works.

The format of a written memoir creates an artificial template for how we think about its author's past:
They generally begin with an attention-grabbing high (or low) point then work backwards to explain how it came to pass.

At Work With:
Shahira Fahmy

How did one of Egypt's leading architects end up walking the red carpet at Cannes?

Words by *Rima Sabina Aouf*
Photography by *Marsý Hild Þórsdóttir*

CHANGE

At 40, Shahira Fahmy took her first acting class. At 43, she walked the Cannes red carpet for the premiere of her first feature film—the French/Korean drama *Claire's Camera* in which she played opposite Isabelle Huppert. Her story of risk and reward is remarkable, even more so because Fahmy already had a successful career, and one that she enjoyed. As an architect, she had her own practice in Cairo, several projects to her name, a teaching post at Columbia University and frequent speaking engagements. Then a set design project sparked her curiosity about acting, and she slowly explored it—to the surprise and, sometimes, disdain of other architects. Now 45, Fahmy is in the middle of another upheaval, as she moves from her near-lifelong home of Cairo to London. Sitting among the packing boxes, she talks about the similarities between acting and architecture and how uncertainty brings opportunity.

RSA: *You had an established career as an architect before you began acting. Why the change?* **SF:** I had a friend who was writing her first feature film and she said, "I want you to design my set, and I'll send you the script." This was the trigger. I read the script and thought, "I want to act in this." She had the lead actress, so I couldn't say "I want to be the lead instead of this girl." But I stayed with her for two, three years, watching actors doing readings, watching cinematographers, reading scripts, and she opened the door to a new world to me. She was learning too, because she came from an art background and had never really studied film. So she was taking these acting classes. And after three years, I went to her acting coach and I got the courage to ask him, "Can you teach me?"

RSA: *When did you start to think this was something you might be good at?* **SF:** After four sessions with this tutor, we had a coffee and he said to me, "You can act." I said, "But you haven't seen anything yet! We've only done voice." He said, "You have a presence and all it takes is a presence."

RSA: *You then interned with the Wooster Group theater company in New York rather than going straight into acting classes. Why?* **SF:** I wanted to tread softly. I wanted to watch things. I wanted to see, Do I want this? Or maybe do I want to work behind the camera? I wanted to be a bit slow about it.

RSA: *It's interesting because we think of internships as something that only young people do.* **SF:** Everybody around me was young.

RSA: *How did that feel?* **SF:** I was okay with it! It was fun because it took me out of my space.

RSA: *Was it hard to go back to being on the bottom of the ladder and taking orders all day?* **SF:** But people don't do that, because they see you. They understand they're talking to a grown-up. When they ask you for something, they will know that you can deliver it, or they will tell you with a certain respect. I had a great time being an intern because it went from answering phones to sewing [costumes] to being the AD [assistant director] and being asked for things that are very important in the production.

RSA: *In 2014, you were awarded Harvard University's Loeb Fellowship, which supports architects' sabbaticals, and that's when you took your acting classes. How necessary was it to take a complete break to make this change?* **SF:** It was very important. I was very focused that I was going to go back to school. And this was a gift, that I had a sabbatical for two years from architecture.

RSA: *Are there lessons or perspectives from architecture that help you in your acting, or vice versa?* **SF:** For me, they are both forms of watching. They are the outcome of watching, they are the performance of watching. I was always interested in people, and watching them is part of the success of the project. You have to have good communication with the team you're working with for it to succeed. If you don't have enough time to really give them attention, the project will fail. It's not all about good design—it's about a good team, from the client to the collaborators to the consultant. I watched a lot when I was a child because I was very shy. During lunches, dinners, all the social things, I was often silent. I was the one who listened and watched.

RSA: *We've talked about age a few times in this conversation. I'd like to hear how your perception of age and aging has changed as you've gotten older.* **SF:** I read once that Carl Jung said that before 40, all your life is research and your life begins at 40. I was very happy reading that line because it felt that way for me. And it resonated with me also because I grew up as a Muslim—not very religious, but Muslim—and 40 in Islam is a big number too. It has meaning in the Quran. So I heard it from two different ends, and it made me feel at peace. Like, okay, I'm just starting.

RSA: *You've lived in Cairo nearly your whole life. The common wisdom is that in times of political upheaval, people crave safety and comfort in their personal lives. It doesn't seem like that's been the case for you?* **SF:** I felt like it's a lost cause, so let's break it all! [laughs] Times of turmoil are the best time to change. Like, I've come here now to London and Brexit. This is the best time; I've learned that from Egypt. The best time to find opportunities is in times of unknowns. When there is uncertainty, then you can maybe make something happen. But if everything is very structured, how can you break in? How can you arrive? How can you change something when it's so stagnant? When the ground is shifting, you should shift yourself.

RSA: *What lessons have you learned over the last few years that might guide other people who are thinking about making big changes?* **SF:** I've started to think of life as something I'm collaborating with. Now and then I have to be silent and listen to what it wants and where it wants to take me and why. I used to have more structure; I knew where I was going. Now I have a lot of unknowns. And in the beginning, that was unsettling. Now I'm happier with having unknowns, and I feel the scary thing is to have a lot of things very known.

> *"I read once that Carl Jung said that before 40, all your life is research. I was very happy reading that line because it felt that way for me."*

As an architect, Fahmy worked exclusively in the MENA region until the Arab Spring, when regional work tapered off and she sought out projects in Switzerland and the UK.

They're too big for their boots, and raiding your closet. Photography by Luc Braquet & Styling by Camille-Joséphine Teisseire

Hair: Taan Doan, Styling Assistant: Céline Gaulhiac

Below: Oliver wears a turtleneck by Ralph Lauren, socks by Falke and shoes by J.M. Weston. Left: Charline wears a turtleneck by Samsøe & Samsøe, socks by Falke and shoes by Zadig & Voltaire. Previous spread: Artur wears a coat by Garçons Infidèles, a sweater by Eric Bompard, trousers by Roseanna and a beret by Rochas.

Above Left: Charline wears a dress by Givenchy. Above Right: June wears a turtleneck by Eric Bompard, socks by Falke and boots by J.M. Weston.
Right: June wears a jacket by Polo Ralph Lauren, a shirt by Uniqlo, belt by Dior and boots by Roseanna.

4.

Directory

178 – 192

Peer Review

An ode to Brazilian novelist *Clarice Lispector*,
by award-winning author (and avid fan) David Keenan.

ÁGUA VIVA

by David Keenan

Água Viva, published in 1973, is Clarice Lispector's holy book, and euphorically so. The book is an incantatory monologue that reads the ordinary and the divine in the same terms in order to come face-to-face with the immanence of God. In *Água Viva*, Lispector uses language upon language to render language null. She has found her element, which was always watery, and flowing, and dangerous in its ability to penetrate everywhere. *Água Viva* is a full-on assault on the present, and so timeless in its range.

Clarice Lispector, the Ukrainian-born Brazilian novelist and short-story writer, arrived fully formed. Her debut novel, the astonishing *Near to the Wild Heart*, was published in 1943 when she was only 23 years old.

The book cribs its title from James Joyce and, like Joyce, Lispector believed in the possibility of epiphany through language—that it is possible to enter into a profound form of communion with it, a sort of deeper knowing.

A Breath of Life, published posthumously and never completed in her lifetime, is the oddest book ever written about the act of writing, about how writing actually *feels* when you are inside it, as well as the responsibilities and complexes that it evokes. For me, writing has always been akin to a state of possession, and Lispector captures that feeling of being overwhelmed by your own creation.

All Lispector books feel like one story, unfolding, and a form of open-heart autobiography. For example, in *The Passion According to* G.H., a Brazilian sculptor crushes a cockroach in a cupboard door and experiences a full-blown spiritual crisis: "We are creatures that must plunge into the depth in order to breathe there, as the fish plunges into the water in order to breathe, except my depths are in the air of the night."

As such, describing the plot of a Lispector novel can be pointless and of no interest: *The Besieged City*, for example, published for the first time in English translation this year, is the story of a young woman who sounds the topography of a city by seeing it and becoming it, through animals, through a geometry of streets, through relationships of soul.

But the magic of her novels is there in the way the language unfolds, and in the presence of Lispector. It's there in every haunted phrase, every bit of uncanny grammar, in its fluctuating tense, in its unparalleled ability to access the now, as if the moment, truly, was a word-besieged outpost and we were somehow, against all odds, breaking through.

A timely history of the alarm clock.

KATIE CALAUTTI

Object Matters

It's no surprise that civilizations across the globe have relied on tricks and gadgets to rise and shine. If there's one constant that has vexed people through the centuries, it's how hard it is to wake up.

Back in the fourth century B.C., Plato used a modified clepsydra—water clock—to wake himself and his students for dawn lectures. In 245 B.C., Ctesibius of Alexandria upgraded the clepsydra into a mechanical version that whistled at a specific time. Then in the eighth century A.D., Chinese engineer Yi Xing rang a decidedly poetic note with his planet, star and time-measuring water wheel clock, which boasted gears that set off puppet shows and gongs.

Ordinary people relied on more rudimentary methods of awakening. In early Christian and Islamic societies, religious bells and chimes in town squares were used to rouse the populace for prayer. During the Industrial Revolution, factories sounded whistles to wake employees who lived within walking distance. For the rest, a new niche profession emerged: knocker-uppers.

Wielding anything from hammers to peashooters to long poles, these entrepreneurs were hired to bang on workers' doors and windows until they got out of bed.

American Levi Hutchins invented his own personal mechanical alarm clock in 1787. His gear-fitted pine box served one unyielding function—to wake him at 4 o'clock every morning. Almost a century later, in 1876, the Seth Thomas Clock Company patented the first fully customizable wind-up version. From there, the alarm clock was sent into mass production, with innovations like travel clocks and radio alarms paving the way for more modern models through the mid-20th century.

Since the advent of the snooze button in the early 1950s, digital clocks and now smartphones have become the alarm of choice. But analog versions have left an indelible mark: As an homage to the snooze feature, which was standardized at nine minutes based on the limitations of mechanical clocks' gear workings, digital and phone app snoozes still default to a nine-minute setting.

Bad Idea: Disposable Clothes

A recollection of the terrible trend for paper dresses.

America in the 1960s was a wild place for lifestyle ideas. People demanded convenience above all else, achievable via newfangled modern technologies: Salad could be made in advance and kept fresh—sort of—by adding Jell-O. Playing fields didn't need to be watered if they were made of plastic ChemGrass (now known as AstroTurf). Best of all, the banality of wearing the same well-made, long-lasting garments year after year could be history with the decade's most bizarre forgotten bad idea: disposable paper clothes.

After the Second World War, it seemed like the mistakes, limitations and hassles of the past could be simply sloughed off and left behind. A 1955 *Life* magazine cover depicting a white, blond nuclear family delightedly flinging disposable objects into the air (something today known as "littering") predicted a celebratory future free from maintenance drudgery. These days, of course, the image reads as foreboding, not fun. As the '50s became the '60s, mundane chores like cleaning, laundry and even cooking seemed laughably antiquated. When they were introduced as a marketing gimmick in 1966 by the toilet paper giant Scott Paper Company, paper clothes scratched a zeitgeisty itch. Scott's dresses, available in two garish prints for $1.25 each, sold 500,000 units in eight months.

For a few years, all the mod young things snapped up paper evening gowns, bell-bottom jumpsuits, Kabuki slippers, bras and bikinis—all designed to be discarded after up to three uses. One extraordinary dress was designed to fit a bride and three bridesmaids at once.

Many of the clothes were treated with fire-retardant chemicals and were partially waterproofed, to forestall the indelicate—not to mention dangerous—eventualities of combining paper with cigarettes, or a rainy day. Another paper dress, implanted with seeds, would burst into bloom when watered.

Like so many ill-considered trends of the 1960s (asbestos, anyone?), the fad soon passed out of favor. But it was a harbinger of a mentality that may yet destroy us. Sadly for the prospect of our planet, our entitlement to disposable convenience is still very much *au courant*.

GOOD IDEA

by Harriet Fitch Little

Fashioning dresses out of paper sounds positively pedestrian compared to some of the materials designers are experimenting with today. Lotus and nettle fibers are catching up with hemp as environmentally friendly alternatives to water-guzzling cotton. Meanwhile, banana plants, pineapple leaves and even apple pulp have all been used to create a host of "vegan leather" materials. But the intention behind these projects is anything but throwaway: The explosion in unusual natural fabrics is part of a push to make the fashion industry more sustainable. Right now, prices mean they're more Harrods than high street, but even the best (or worst) ideas have to start somewhere.

Photograph: Cecilie Jegsen

JAMES CLASPER

Last Night

What did Danish design gallerist *Rune Bruun Johansen* do with his evening?

Rune Bruun Johansen, 44, is a furniture designer and Nordic modern furniture dealer based in Copenhagen. He has designed pieces for the Danish prime minister's official residence and worked with chef Frederik Bille Brahe to redesign the Apollo Bar and Kantine at Kunsthal Charlottenborg.

JC: *How much sleep did you get last night?* **RBJ:** About three to five hours. I have a newborn son and he was awake most of the night.

JC: *How much did you want to get?* **RBJ:** A few more hours. I normally sleep six to eight. But I'm not a big sleeper and don't take naps.

JC: *What did you do with your evening?* **RBJ:** We went for a long walk with the stroller around the lakes and the park, just talking about life, and then bought groceries.

JC: *What do you keep on your bedside table?* **RBJ:** Too many things. It's a mess. Everything from my pockets—bills, coins, keys—and a watch. I also have a photograph of my girlfriend when she was a child and a drawing that my daughter made for me. I'm very much into poetry and just gave my girlfriend a book of poems by Inger Christensen. We also have a book about the Chelsea Hotel in New York.

JC: *When did you last stay up all night?* **RBJ:** My friend's wedding about a year and a half ago. I was the best man with two other guys and we stayed up long after dawn

JC: *What's the best place you've spent the night?* **RBJ:** Architect Tadao Ando's Benesse House Oval, on the Japanese island of Naoshima. It was so beautiful. Also, my father and I slept in a monastery on the Greek peninsula of Athos, and were woken by bells.

JC: *And the strangest?* **RBJ:** When I was 18, on the floor of my friend the photographer Thomas Loof's apartment in Chinatown, in New York, with mice running around me.

In 2015, Johansen relocated his gallery into the same 18th-century rococobuilding in Copenhagen that houses Design Museum Denmark.

Cult Rooms

Few rooms loom as large in the popular psyche as the shrink's office. *Stephanie d'Arc Taylor considers the couch where it all began.*

Lie back, close your eyes and conjure a scene of psychoanalysis. Most likely, a couch is there, in the middle of an expensive-looking office. The first person to come to mind (after your therapist, if you have one) might be Woody Allen. Or, perhaps, a 60-something white man stroking his beard, looking inquisitive and vaguely alarmed.

The therapeutic couch was first utilized in the 1890s by Sigmund Freud, the Austrian founder of psychoanalysis (and archetype of our beardy, bespectacled intellectual above). Since then, the humble piece of furniture has become so associated with psychotherapy that the phrase "on the couch" has come to signify the practice. But the couch has traditionally been more a means to an end, rather than something valuable in itself, says Dr. Mark Gerald on the phone from his practice in, yes, New York. Gerald interviewed and photographed over 100 psychoanalysts all over the world for his book *In the Shadow of Freud's Couch: Portraits of Psychoanalysts in Their Offices* (Routledge, 2019).

In years past, an analyst's office was a reflection of his particular methodology. Disciples of the Swiss psychiatrist Carl Jung, for instance, modeled their offices after the Greek idea of *temenos*, or interior holy sanctuary, thought to incubate mental labor. Freudian analysts kept their offices free from any traces of personality: "The non-intrusion of the analyst, and the non-person-al effects in the office, was considered instrumental to the release of the more unconscious parts of the patient's mind," says Gerald. (The Freudian approach is, notably, different from that of Freud himself, who kept many objects of personal significance in his office, including paintings, photographs and statuary.)

In the first modern analyst's office of Gilded Age Vienna, the couch was there to a similar end: keeping the patient's mind on itself and off the analyst. (Legend has it that Freud originally turned the couch away from his chair after a recumbent patient tried to seduce him.) Traditionally, "psychoanalysis has privileged hearing over seeing," confirms Gerald. This set in motion what he describes as "an averting of the eyes, a kind of blindness" between patient and analyst. This, of course, is an impossible task, even for an analyst. "Showing oneself is not really even a conscious choice," says Gerald. "It's inevitable."

These days, your therapist would probably be concerned if you plopped down and stretched out —if she even has a couch at all. Over the 20th century, the couch fell out of favor as the discipline of psychotherapy came under the same scrutiny as many other schools of social science. The emphasis of psychoanalysis, Gerald says, shifted from what's "taking place only inside the patient's mind, to recognizing that it's a relational matrix going on all the time between the two parties in

Freud and his family moved to London in 1938 to escape Nazi persecution. The residence is now open as a museum, and the some 2,000 items that filled his study have been left as they were in his lifetime.

the room." So how is this shift in theory reflected in the modern analyst aesthetic? Today's analysts, says Gerald, look a lot more like, well, themselves. "Using all of oneself in the work includes how one dresses, and what is shown in the physical space," he says. Through his research, he saw that there isn't a typical analyst's office today: "The individual aesthetic becomes what's important." In Gerald's own practice, personal objets have led to breakthroughs with his patients; he speaks with great reverence, in particular, of a miniature tennis racket he bought one year at the U.S. Open.

The image of a wizened European gentleman with deeply furrowed brows is as much a part of the psychoanalyst's office trope as the couch: a Freud figure appears in nearly every *New Yorker* cartoon on the subject, of which there are many. But this stereotype has had its day, and good riddance, says Gerald. "I'm especially interested in showing the face of psychoanalysis today, and challenging the stereotype that it's a deadened practice occupied by old white men," he says. Rather than focusing on any one orthodox method, or aesthetic, individuality in psychoanalysis is now not only accepted, but celebrated. "People entering the field today are primarily women from diverse backgrounds," says Gerald. "The common thread now is the protection and appreciation of the unconscious world." *Photograph: Freud Museum London*

The keeper of Copenhagen's veterinary collection has a two-headed calf and a bisected lion in her collection. She talks to *James Clasper* about why she feels like Indiana Jones.

JAMES CLASPER

Annika Normann

JC: *You must have one of the most unusual jobs in Copenhagen. Tell me about it.* **AN:** I'm a natural history conservator. I look after the historical collections of veterinary and animal science at the University of Copenhagen. Most people think I'm a taxidermist, because it's the same word in Danish. Much of my work involves changing the fluid that preserves the "wet specimens" in the collections and registering them clearly.

JC: *How old are the collections?* **AN:** The specimens date mainly from the 1800s, with a few from the early 1900s and some were even collected by Peter Christian Abildgaard, who founded the School of Veterinary Medicine in 1773. I'm the first person to work with most of the collections for about 30 years. Much of it was scattered all over the campus and moved into basements, attics and so on. In fact, my master's thesis involved working out what was where, and how much was left. I was handed a campus master key, and I could get into all rooms to look for lost museum objects—I felt very much like Indiana Jones.

JC: *How big are the collections, and what's in them?* **AN:** There are 11 veterinary collections, and we've counted about 37,000 specimens and items. For instance, there's a collection of various medical instruments that were used to heal animals, a parasitical collection, a zoological and an anatomical collection, which was used to teach veterinary students about the healthy animal before they learnt how to treat sick animals, and a pathological collection, where you can see animals that had deformities, diseases, or injuries like broken bones.

JC: *That sounds macabre.* **AN:** Not if you see the purpose of the collection. It's not meant to be a freak show—it was an educational tool, made to support the curriculum. Today the collections are also important in terms of cultural history. This is one of the world's oldest veterinary schools, so there's a rich history.

JC: *Has your work changed how you think about death?* **AN:** It probably has. I don't know. The dead animals in our collection served an important purpose, which was to educate future veterinarians, therefore hopefully saving the lives of other animals.

Some people on social media don't always see it that way. For example, I recently put up a cross section of a reptile's guts and a woman wrote to say she hoped the same thing would happen to me.

JC: *You now have 18,000 followers on Instagram. What do you post, and why?* **AN:** We don't have a museum, so it's really my only way to show people what I do and how much work we put into it. I also post to push people a bit. The pathology collection has things like two-headed calves. Some people are really into that. But you have to pique people's interest with something that looks a bit weird, so they think, "Oh my God, what is that?" and then hopefully they'll read the explanatory text that I spent three hours writing.

JC: *Which specimens do you find particularly interesting?* **AN:** Some of the cross sections of mammals, like the lion's head, where you can see its tongue, jaw and nasal cavity. You don't always know what it is, but it's just so beautiful. Maybe because it's another way of seeing the animal and you can see how everything works and where everything is placed. Back then, this was all they had. They didn't have 3D scans or YouTube videos. The professors spent hours on each specimen. Some are very artistic, almost like abstract paintings.

JC: *Or like Damien Hirst's sharks in formaldehyde.* **AN:** Yes, his work is amazing. We don't have the capacity to have big animals, but it would be nice to have a pony or perhaps a whole cat.

JC: *You would have the ultimate cat photo for Instagram.* **AN:** Yes, we would!

ANNA GUNDLACH

Crossword

ACROSS

1. Kind of soda
5. Settled a debt
9. Three Little Pigs material
14. Fashion designer Sui
15. Adjective on a shoppe sign
16. Put back on the air
17. Snitch, in slang
18. Cocktail garnish
19. Ballerina's support
20. I originally wrote one clue here, but for a change of pace, the new clue is "What a mollusk uses to keep its shell dry?"
23. Shriek from a kid who hasn't learned to share
24. Didn't give up on
25. Tool that helps prepare plots
27. Big name in inspirational talks
28. Baseball hall-of-famer Mel
29. After a change of gear, I've decided the new clue here is "Anger at people who leave their garbage all over the forest?"
33. Francophonic "thanks"
34. Bottled spirit
35. Indian royal
38. Dancer's lead?
41. Put one's foot down
42. Latin phrase of explanation
44. Deck with Judgement and The Tower
46. I've had a change of heart, and the new clue here is "What's left over after an archaeological dig?"
49. A long way
52. Nurse
53. Postal creed conjunction
54. Do harm to
56. Drive like a maniac
58. There's been a change of course, and the new clue here is "15th century Scotland?"
61. Scandalous company of 2001
63. Train sound
64. Retirement options
65. Thus
66. 2019 #1 album by Tyler, the Creator
67. Recovering dog's accessory
68. Entered (in)
69. Wyoming town named for Buffalo Bill
70. Ma'ams with rams and lambs

DOWN

1. Comfortable clog company
2. Caught like a butterfly
3. Totally engrossed
4. Not needing to be said
5. Beyoncé, Rihanna, et al.
6. Actor who played Obi-Wan
7. Piece of mind?
8. Oracle's locale
9. "c u soon"
10. Printer's quantity
11. Sand, to a pearl oyster
12. Famous philanthropist
13. Really in the thick of
21. Some goth clothing material
22. A billion years
26. Play a Halloween prank on
30. Longtime record label
31. Part of a sea-faring trio
32. Sign for a musician to not play
33. End-of-the-day skin care option
35. Bone-in beef cut
36. Feminist poet Rich who said "When a woman tells the truth she is creating the possibility for more truth around her"
37. Game show that raises many questions
39. Roofing material
40. Adept creativity
43. Hamilton
45. "That's not good at all..."
47. Holiday beverage
48. Steamy, like some fiction
49. Scrunch up, like one's brow
50. Understood by a select few
51. Cups and Pieces brand
55. It's in batteries, figuratively
57. Romantic gift
59. Interlocking LV, for example
60. You can't live without it
62. Silent affirmation

DAPHNÉE DENIS

Correction

Why catchy health guidelines require careful examination.

Eat five portions of fruits and vegetables a day. Walk 10,000 steps. Drink eight glasses of water. Sleep eight consecutive hours a night. These magic numbers are meant to keep us healthy. In order to optimize our well-being, smart apps track our hydration levels, our intake of greens, our sleep and, of course, our every step. Yet, supposed benefits aside, these targets have one thing in common: They all have their origins in marketing strategy—and in one case, a workers' rights campaign—rather than science.

The five-a-day slogan, championed by the British government in 2003 and embraced worldwide to encourage healthier eating habits, does not suggest the ideal daily amount of fruits and vegetables we should have. Rather, it is based on the 400 grams recommended by the World Health Organization as the *minimum* daily intake for the prevention of chronic diseases. Campaigners landed on five-a-day because "achievable" matters more than "ideal" when it comes to effective public health campaigning.

The 10,000-step myth has far stranger origins. It dates back to the 1960s, when a Japanese company started marketing a pedometer called manpo-kei—the "10,000 steps meter." Even though walking more does lower mortality rates, a recent study by Harvard's School of Public Health found that we really just need to walk up to 7,500 steps a day. Its lead researcher believes the 10,000 objective was arbitrarily picked because the Japanese sign for it resembles a man walking.

Water is a component of many fluids and foods, which means how much of it we need to drink varies according to what else we consume and how much we sweat. The eight hours of sleep rule is a product of the Industrial Revolution, when workers found that they could make a neat case for a shorter work day by insisting that every 24-hour period should be divided into eight hours of labor, eight hours of leisure and eight hours of rest, in order to limit their work days.

Quantifying our well-being with easy-to-remember rules may be reassuring, but remember to keep an open mind: The most useful health guidelines aren't always those with the snappiest slogans.

Easy-to-remember advice is appealing: Health authorities recommend drinking eight 8-ounce glasses of water each day, a formula that has been given the memorable moniker of the 8×8 rule.

Stockists

A.P.C.
apc.fr

ACNE STUDIOS
acnestudios.com

ALEXANDER MCQUEEN
alexandermcqueen.com

AMI PARIS
amiparis.com

ARIEL GORDON
arielgordonjewelry.com

AESOP
aesop.com

CALVIN KLEIN
calvinklein.com

CASSINA
cassina.com

CECILIE BAHNSEN
ceciliebahnsen.com

CHARLOTTE CHESNAIS
charlottechesnais.fr

CHRISTIAN WIJNANTS
christianwijnants.com

COS
cosstores.com

DAKS
daks.com

DE FURSAC
defursac.fr

DIOR
dior.com

ECKHAUS LATTA
eckhauslatta.com

EQUIPMENT
equipmentfr.com

ERIC BOMPARD
eric-bompard.com

ERIK JOERGENSEN
erik-joergensen.com

FALKE
falke.com

GARÇONS INFIDÈLES
garconsinfideles.com

GIVENCHY
givenchy.com

HAAT
isseymiyake.com/haat

HELMUT LANG
helmutlang.com

HERMÈS
hermes.com

HOUSE OF FINN JUHL
finnjuhl.com

INABO
inabo.se

J.M. WESTON
jmweston.com

JENNIFER FISHER
jenniferfisherjewelry.com

KIKO KOSTADINOV
kikokostadinov.com

LADY GREY
ladygreyjewelry.com

LOCK & CO
lockhatters.co.uk

LOUIS VUITTON
louisvuitton.com

LUDOVIC DE SAINT SERNIN
ludovicdesaintsernin.com

MAISON MARGIELA
maisonmargiela.com

MARIMEKKO
marimekko.com

MARSET
marset.com

MARYAM NASSIR ZADEH
mnzstore.com

MAX MARA
maxmara.com

MIU MIU
miumiu.com

MOON CHOI
moonchoistudio.com

MULBERRY
mulberry.com

NOMOS
nomos-glashuette.com

OFF-WHITE
off---white.com

ORIOR
oriorfurniture.com

PARACHUTE HOME
parachutehome.com

PORTUGUESE FLANNEL
portugueseflannel.com

PYER MOSS
pyermoss.com

RALPH LAUREN
ralphlauren.com

ROCHAS
rochas.com

ROSEANNA
roseanna.fr

SAINT LAURENT
ysl.com

SALVATORE FERRAGAMO
ferragamo.com

SAMSØE & SAMSØE
samsoe.com

STAUD
staud.clothing

STRING
stringfurniture.com

TIBI
tibi.com

UNIQLO
uniqlo.com

VALENTINO
valentino.com

WALES BONNER
walesbonner.net

ZADIG & VOLTAIRE
zadig-et-voltaire.com

Credits

COVER
Photographer
Romain Laprade
Stylist
Camille-Joséphine Teisseire
Groomer
Giulio Panciera
Model
Kaissan Ibrahima at SUPA
Model Management
Location
Les Jardins de Marqueyssac,
France

Kaissan wears a silk shirt
by Hermès and trousers
by Palla.

P. 18
Photograph first published
in Extraordinary Friends,
St. Martin's Press, 1993.

P. 30
Photograph: Tree #14 by
Myoung Ho Lee, 2009. ©
Myoung Ho Lee. Courtesy
of Yossi Milo Gallery, New
York.

P. 36
Makeup
Lucas Lisboa
Model
Nabillah Sedar

P. 42-51
Set Design
Javier Irigoyen
Hair
Eloise Cheung
Makeup
Rommy Najor

P. 56-69
Photographer
Romain Laprade
Stylist
Camille-Joséphine Teisseire
Groomer
Giulio Panciera
Model
Kaissan Ibrahima at SUPA
Model Management
Location
Les Jardins de Marqueyssac,
France

P. 104-113
Hair
Tomihiro Kono
Makeup
Agus Suga
Model
Ashika Pratt at Heroes
Models

P. 144-151
Photo Assistant
Benjamin Whitley

P. 162-167
Makeup
Roberta Kearsey

P. 168-176
Models
June Bernard Gourion at
Frimousse
Arthur Bengel at Frimousse
Oliver Poku-Boadum at
Frimousse
Owen Poku-Boadum at
Frimousse
Charline Bridet at Teen

Copenhagen's School of Veterinary Medicine holds over 35,000 specimens; these foal lungs are Normann's favorite item in the collection.

JAMES CLASPER

My Favorite Thing

Annika Normann, keeper of Copenhagen's veterinary collection interviewed on page 185, waxes lyrical about a foal's wax lungs.

My favorite thing in our collection is a waxwork model of an unborn foal's lungs. It was made in 1896 for the anatomical collection at the veterinary school. It's such a delicate and beautiful specimen, and it's amazing how well-developed the foal's lungs are after five months of gestation. It's also a really hard technique and must have taken such a long time to make. The craftsman who made it used wax to fill all the capillaries of the lungs and then different chemicals to remove the soft tissue, so that we are able to see all the bronchial airways. I love that you can see how it was made, and the color of the wax.

You can also see the old label that tells you the name of the craftsman and the professor he made it for. This specimen is meaningful to me and hopefully it can spark an interest in other people as well. It's a good example of how the school taught throughout the years, and hopefully it will be an inspiration for current students as well. Though it was an educational item for veterinarians, it's almost a piece of art. We would not be able to make a specimen like this today.